THE
Quilting Arts
BOOK

Patricia Bolton

INTERWEAVE.
interweavebooks.com

Editor Rebecca Campbell
Cover and Interior Design Connie Poole
Production Designer Katherine Jackson
Cover Photography Joe Coca
Interior Photography Larry Stein and Korday Studios

Text © 2008 Interweave Press LLC
Photography © 2008 Interweave Press LLC
Cover art, clockwise from top left: Angie Hughes, Katie
Korkos, Linda Kemshall, and Leslie Tucker Jenison

Interweave Press LLC
201 East Fourth Street
Loveland, CO 80537-5655 USA
interweavebooks.com

Printed in China by Asia Pacific Offset.

Library of Congress Cataloging-in-Publication Data

Bolton, Patricia.
  The quilting arts book : techniques and inspiration for creating one-of-a-kind art quilts / Patricia Bolton, author.
      p. cm.
  Includes index.
  ISBN 978-1-59668-099-9 (pbk.)
  1. Quilting. 2. Art quilts. I. Title.
  TT835.B51443 2008
  746.46'041--dc22
                          2008014305

10 9 8 7 6 5 4 3 2 1

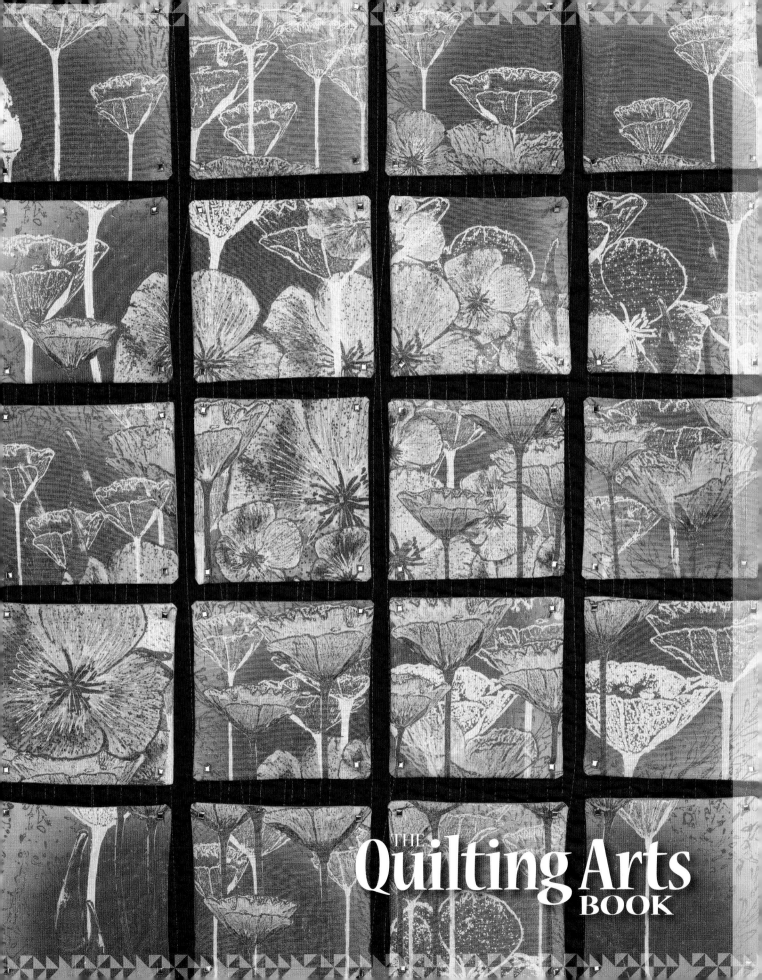

The Quilting Arts
BOOK

Contents

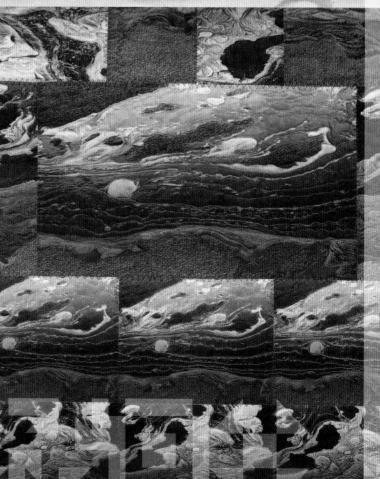

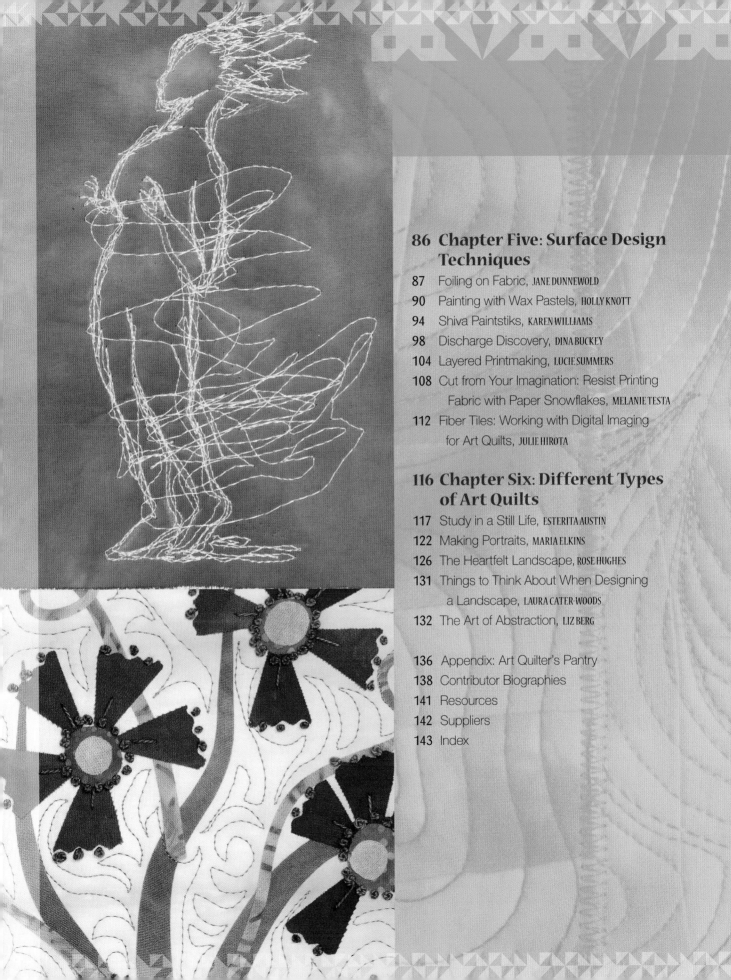

"Grandmother's Lullaby," 45" W x 33" L (114cm x 84cm).

Approximately ten years ago, I walked into a craft store for the first time in my adult life. I had been immersed in graduate school for so long while holding down a day job, I was desperate to put the computer away and create something tangible with my hands. That year my mother had given me some money for Christmas, and, instead of buying yet another winter coat, I decided to learn a new craft. When I walked into that craft store, I was overwhelmed by the choices in front of me. Would I learn to knit, make candles, create papier-mâché? I strolled through the store marveling at all of the striking yarns and the smells of scented candle wax, yet I was lured by the colorful bolts of fabric that lined the back wall. In the end, I chose to quilt.

I first strolled through the books aisle, where I found a beginner book on quilting. I skimmed the pages until I found a materials list and promptly dropped a rotary cutter, cutting mat, threads, batting, fat quarters, threads, and even a sewing machine into my basket. For the next week, while on vacation from both work and school, I turned my dining-room table into a quilting room. With my new quilting book in hand, I strip-pieced brightly hued fabrics together and came away with a rather vibrant (almost too vibrant) quilt that showed I had a lot to learn in order to master the art of quilting.

I spent the next couple of months honing my quilting skills and made a couple of other traditional quilts. As I started to get the hang of it, however, I realized I wanted something more out of fabric and stitch—something more expressive and personal that also incorporated embroidery and embellishment. That's when I stumbled upon crazy quilting and the wonderful world of novelty fabrics, beads, and embellishment. Soon after, in 2000, I left my doctoral program and day job to found *Quilting Arts Magazine*, where I learned, alongside the readership, about embellishing, designing, and creating art out of cloth.

Over the years, *Quilting Arts Magazine* has delved into a variety of topics related to art quilting—art and design principles for fabric artists, embellishment, surface design techniques, free-motion embroidery, and fabric collage, to name just a few. However, I am often asked by people who have never created an art quilt: What one book would I suggest to learn about art quilting?

I present you with this book. Here you'll find a number of favorite articles from past issues of *Quilting Arts Magazine* combined with fresh material to create a comprehensive book with a wealth of information for the budding and intermediate art quilter. With this book the masters in the field give us insight into how they create their art so successfully. With everything from keeping a textile sketchbook to stitching with mixed media, this book is one I hope you can refer to again and again as you grow as a fiber artist.

Happy quilting!

Patricia Bolton
Editor-in-Chief
Quilting Arts Magazine

Chapter One
GETTING STARTED

Ask any award-winning art quilters how they come up with their original designs and they'll tell you that as much as they wish it worked that way, their designs don't simply come to them magically in a dream; rather, the artists spend a lot of time developing and thinking about their designs before they ever pick up a needle. In this chapter, we'll go over the basics to get you started on your art-quilting journey: tips for where and how to find inspiration for your art quilts, reasons keeping a sketchbook is so important, and guidelines for journal quilting to help hone your skills.

Finding Inspiration

Linda and Laura Kemshall

WHERE WE GET THE IDEAS is the question Laura and I are asked more often than any other. There is no single answer to this. Ideas can come at any time and in the strangest places. It is true that sometimes inspiration can strike out of the blue, maybe one of those sleepless middle-of-the-night flashes of genius that, when you think about it again in the cold light of day, isn't always quite as impressive or indeed entirely practical. It would be perfect if we could just dream a great quilt design and wake up the next morning ready to go with it; amazingly that does occasionally happen, but usually it's much more likely that we have to work a little harder than that. Before we can launch ourselves into fabrics and threads, we need an idea with which to work.

Take Time to Think

For us, the initial creative idea that gets the whole thing going is more important to the development of a quilt than the time that will be spent actually making it; it usually takes longer, too. We call this our "thinking time." We plot and plan and ask ourselves: What if? We draw and paint and scribble lists of relevant words onto the pages of our sketchbooks. This brainstorming of words and ideas can happen individually or we can bounce thoughts back and forth between the two of us. Sometimes it's a combination; first we have our individual thoughts and then we run them by each other to see the other's reaction. When you trust another person's judgment, it is such a help. Working on your own can be hard. Whatever happens, it's an invaluable part of the design development; putting thoughts into words crystallizes our vague intentions, making them seem concrete and realistic. Sometimes just telling someone else about an idea can clarify it in your mind and help you decide on the nitty-gritty practicalities involved in making the dream a reality. Once all of the basic design decisions have been made, thinking time is over and the construction process is

A page from one of Laura's quilt books, incorporating digital image transfer, handpainting, and free-motion quilting; the lettering is digitally embroidered.

Crow photo by Phyllis Tarrant.

usually pretty straightforward. Now that we know how the quilt will look and what we want to achieve, we can relax and simply enjoy working with all the fantastic patchwork, appliqué, and quilting techniques we love most.

Detail of Linda's "Home to Roost" quilt, 30" W x 18½" L (76cm x 47cm).

Choose a Subject

Ideas for design can come from almost anywhere. Once you have trained your eyes to see beauty and inspiration in everyday objects and places, it becomes second nature to spot their potential. With quiltmaking, as in all textile arts, most forms of inspiration have a strong visual element. Studying a favorite precious object really closely can be an easy way to develop a completely new design. The elements of design that are needed are simple—color, line, shape, texture, and form. Any object that we find fascinating or beautiful is guaranteed to have enough of those required elements to be used to produce a new design. Laura and I try hard to identify the essential character of what we study. We prefer to produce a design that captures the essence of the object rather than reproducing it literally. This might mean the connection with the source of the design is quite tenuous. For instance, we might just identify the colors involved in the original and use them to create a gorgeous color scheme for a quilt. At other times we might exploit the shapes, lines, and textures found within the source as well as using its color.

Sometimes our inspiration is an event or experience rather than a single object. Choosing a subject that captures the imagination makes the research of the subject enjoyable and rewarding. Routine experiences of daily life or more unusual events, such as a special trip or family celebration, can all be sources of inspiration. We tell our students that as long as they work with an idea or concept that is personal to them and pursue it from their own perspective, they'll produce work that is different and individual regardless of its popularity. Choosing a subject that is close to your heart will ensure your design work reflects that depth of feeling and passion.

Explore Your Theme

Most quilt designs fall into one of two categories: concept-led or process-led. Although processes and products are vital to the success of any quilt, for us and our style of work, ideas have equal value. Technique is simply the vocabulary through which our ideas are interpreted in cloth and stitch. We will always establish the theme or concept, no matter how simple it is, as the first step in the design process. In fact, we usually have the name for the quilt long before the first stitch is even taken. When we take on a brand-new theme, we consider researching and developing our ideas as a journey of discovery and we don't worry too much about the outcome. Anticipating the destination spoils the excitement and mystery of the journey and preempting the outcome of the design process can also limit the potential results. Keeping an open mind, being prepared to experiment, and developing the ability to spot the "happy accident" are very desirable skills and, along with a lifelong curiosity for all things creative, are to be encouraged.

When we have a theme in mind and have brainstormed words to kick-start our ideas we usually take photos, make sketches, and collect images—and sometimes real objects, too. We might also look into how other people have tackled a similar subject. We don't restrict this to artists who work in the field of textiles; indeed, we look more often to fine-art painters for inspiration. Another artist's interpretation of the same theme might be interesting in terms of color palette or from a compositional point of view. By working with recurring favorite themes, revisiting them over a period of time, and blending in other, more recent influences, we make designing an ongoing, organic, and constantly evolving process.

Team Up

The creative process is often a solitary activity, and although as mother and daughter we are lucky to work together on many of our projects, we find that from time to time we really enjoy the opportunity to interact with others. This can be especially productive when developing ideas for new work. Belonging to a quilt group or getting together with a few like-minded individuals to chat and share ideas can often ignite the spark of creativity that is evasive when working in isolation. Group activities can be very informal and spontaneous, but they are probably more successful with a few boundaries. We like to set our group challenges within definite parameters. Whether members of the group intend to contribute to a single collaborative piece or create individual pieces, we provide a specific list of rules. We have found that the quilts produced this way complement each other because of the things they have in common—size, color, theme, and so forth—while remaining completely different because of the personality of the individual maker. It has proved to be a successful way of achieving a cohesive set of quilts for exhibition. A group challenge can be very demanding and even stir a competitive element between the members, but it is usually equally satisfying.

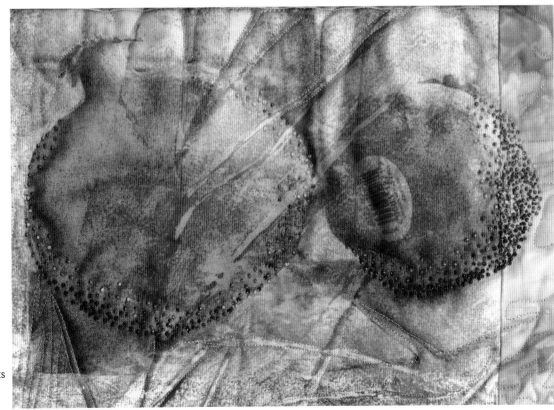

Detail of Linda's "Full and Fine" quilt, 36" W x 16" L (91cm x 41cm), a photographic image transfer on Jacquard's ExtravOrganza, overlaid onto a screen print with embellishments of French knots and beads.

Altered photograph of poppy seed heads.

Set a Goal

We are both driven and committed and have no problem with setting goals for ourselves. Sometimes, though, it can be fun to have external deadlines imposed on us. Competitions and challenges such as those set by a magazine can open up new avenues to explore. By accepting a challenge devised by someone else, you may find that you are tackling something completely new and outside of your normal comfort zone. You might even find that something that initially doesn't fire your enthusiasm will turn out to be thoroughly enjoyable. One of Laura's most productive periods involved working on a series of quilts inspired by poppies. This set of work arose from a competition brief that, at first, she found difficult to come to grips with. In the end it turned out to be one of the most fruitful spells of research and development, leading to more than twenty-five quilts.

Not only may a challenge or competition encourage you to tackle a new theme, it may also require you to work in a format different than your usual approach. If you're a conventional quilter, working in two dimensions, then taking one of your favorite subject themes and working with it to make a wearable item, a doll, or a piece of book art could introduce a whole new perspective. Likewise, if you normally work in a large-scale format, consider entering a competition for miniature patchwork and quilting.

Engage the Muses

We all work in a visual medium, be it pieced, quilted, embroidered, or painted, but our sources of inspiration need not always be visual. Sometimes work can reflect a personal response to an emotion, to the spoken or written word, or to the lyrics of a song. The work that results from these more intangible sources of inspiration may be completely abstract or you might illustrate the meaning of the words much as an artist illustrates a storybook, in a more figurative and immediately recognizable way, so that anyone familiar with your source of inspiration would recognize the connection you are making. It's fascinating to discover that, in all creative arts, be they visual, literary, or musical, the same principles of design apply—they're just involved in a slightly different form. We talk about harmonious color, regular pattern, and balanced composition in a quilt design. Listening to music, you become aware of the rhythms of the sounds and the harmonious or discordant qualities of the notes. Repeating certain passages of music or lines of songs creates patterns and rhythms within the verses and chorus of the song. If you want to find out how influential music can be on your mood, take a paintbrush and a couple of generous pots of paint and begin applying color to a large sheet of paper while music plays loudly in the background. What kind of music are you listening to? Is it encouraging broad, expansive movements of your entire arm or just tiny little movements of your fingers? Are the marks you make fluid or angular, curved or straight? The sounds you hear can influence which colors you choose as well as how you place them. The highs and lows of the melody, the phrasing and organization of the words could all inspire and influence a quilting design. How about taking a favorite poem or verse and reading it out loud to yourself until you create mental images suggested by the words? How might you recreate those images on cloth?

One way to work out these questions and to experiment with materials and techniques is to use a sketchbook.

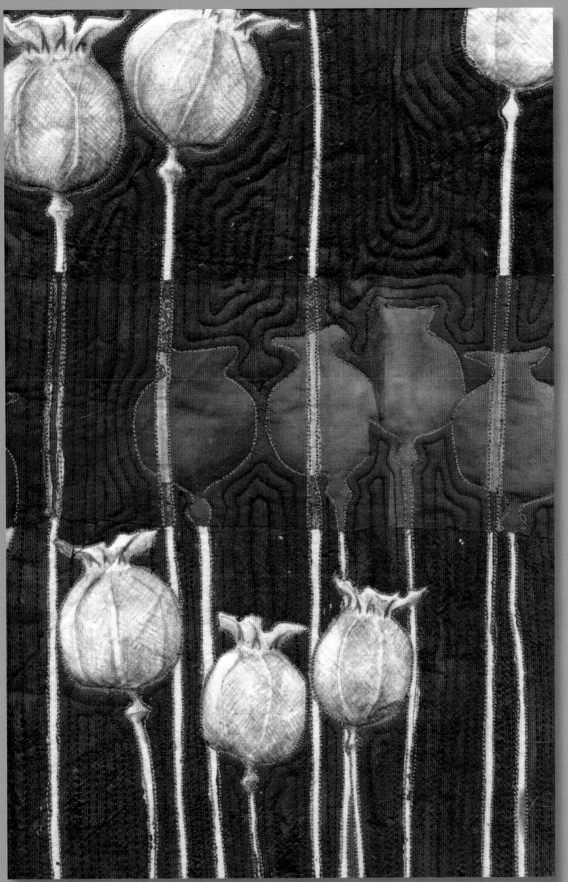

A detail from Laura's quilt "Morpheus's Garden," 39" x 39" (99cm x 99cm), inspired by poppy seed heads.

A sketchbook page of poppies using acrylic paint, applied with a palette knife.

Keeping a Sketchbook
Linda and Laura Kemshall

MOST PEOPLE WHO MAKE QUILTS do so perfectly well without reference to a sketchbook. So you might ask the question: Why would a quilter want to keep a sketchbook at all? Quilts are a visual art form and ideas for designs are usually found in a visual form. For many, that inspiration can be found in magazines and books, not only in those publications devoted to quiltmaking techniques, but also in any that include images of interesting subjects, beautiful compositions, or glorious and unusual color combinations. Of course, quilters might also choose to take a traditional quilt design and play with the colors and value placements until they make the design entirely their own. They may be talented enough to do that intuitively or they may prefer to rely on a computer program to speed the process along.

What if you want to make a truly original design to celebrate a special trip, record a fascinating object you've seen, or immortalize something that captures your imagination in your everyday life? We tend to work from these very immediate sources of inspiration ourselves—objects or places that we see every day and things that are important to us and probably found close to home. The best way we know to record what we see so that we will be able to work on it to develop a design is to photograph and draw it. Keeping a sketchbook is like keeping a diary—it needs to be added to regularly, or it will be incomplete and lack continuity. Regular practice in recording visual ideas leads to an increased confidence with the process of design, and that familiarity and ease encourages creativity. The sketchbook does not have to be technically perfect. For design purposes, it is a means to an artistic end and not the end in itself.

How to Start

Sketchbooks can be bought in a wide range of sizes and formats. Choose one with a shape and proportion you find appealing. It is a very personal choice. I like to use spiral-bound books that open out completely flat when I work in them, but Laura feels the metal binding interrupts the visual flow of the open spread and prefers hardback books with stitched spines. With these she can draw, print, and paint across the join as though it didn't exist, altering the proportion of the page and making full use of the available space. We both like square books, but sometimes the themes we explore suggest that a landscape or portrait format would be more suitable. We always have several sketchbooks on the go at any time so we can switch from one to another, although if we're honest, that's more because we're too impatient for the pages to dry than for any artistic reason. What's more important than the shape of the book is the paper quality. If you intend to use media such as acrylic paint, ink, and watercolor, the paper must be heavy enough to accept the wet color without buckling and rippling. It is very frustrating to have poor quality, thin paper that isn't robust enough to take what we throw at it! We may intend a distressed effect eventually, but we don't want the paper to fall apart before we achieve it.

Altered Alternatives

Many people find the pristine perfection of the blank page intimidating. For them, altering an existing book might work. Almost any book can be altered by painting on the pages, adding drawings and text, and even stitching sections of pages together. Large-format children's storybooks can be exciting to work with and usually don't have as many pages to deal with. If you can find a book with a theme that's relevant to your current inspiration, it's fun to focus attention on sections of text or images by highlighting them or by painting out surrounding distractions before adding your own contributions. A sketchbook to record a special journey or holiday

Linda's oil pastel and watercolor wash sketchbook pages with punching and eyelets.

Linda's acrylic prints and oil pastel wash with bleach drawings.

might be perfect worked onto an old atlas, for instance. If the book is purely for your own satisfaction, it's probably okay to cannibalize anything that comes to hand, but if you intend to exhibit your altered book, make sure that you are not infringing copyright laws.

Journals

Treating your sketchbook like a diary or journal is a great way of bringing many disparate elements together in a thoughtful way. Although this technique often relies heavily on collage, we try to avoid a scrappy effect by integrating the bits and pieces fully with the page itself. The easiest way to do this is to identify the colors and textures of the ephemera and apply a wash of color to the page before gluing the ticket stub or scrap of road map to it. If the image has interesting lines or shapes, these can be isolated and used to decorate the page or extend the image across selected areas of the journal page. Repeating an element or extending a line creates visual continuity and doesn't have to stop at the edge of the page—we sometimes take a stamped shape or a drawn line around and onto the following or preceding page. This is an excellent way to lead the eye of the viewer in a particular direction and can suggest the work has a narrative quality.

Where to Begin?

If you've never kept a sketchbook or visual diary, start now! Aim to add to it regularly. Save interesting scraps that catch your eye, stamps from exotic foreign places, labels, photographs, textile samples, and fabric swatches. These can be the basic ingredients of your book, and you can add to them with any media and technique you wish. Just like us, you might begin with good intentions to keep the sketchbook organized and centered on just one theme, but our books never stay that way for long. We're impatient, so pages can occasionally get slightly stuck together; generous, so color seeps through to the next page; and impulsive, so we'll tear out sections of pages that aren't working, or begin a totally different train of thought right in the middle of something else. Gather together any ephemera that you want to use and start by sticking it to the pages. Treat the photos as areas of color and pattern. Draw on them, cut into them, and really try to integrate them to the page. What you do with what you've collected, with the marks you make, the way you collage, cut, and paint, will be making an important statement about what you've observed.

Adding Color

We recommend that you always buy the best quality of art materials you can afford. They'll be expensive, but you can save money by purchasing just the basic paint and pastels in primary colors and learning to mix the colors you need. You'll find mixing and layering color to create your own combinations and hues most satisfying, and with practice you'll be able to quickly mix the color you really need. Artist-quality paints yield colors that are more luscious and intense than the cheaper student-quality ranges. Approach shopping in the art-supply store just as you would in a fabric shop. Isn't it better to have just a little piece of gorgeous fabric in a couple of colors than yards and yards of cheap fabric that will let your work down no matter how hard you try?

Making Marks

Drawing can seem like a scary thing to start with, but don't be nervous. Your sketchbook is your private place to try things out. No one else need see your efforts unless you want them to. A pencil is an accessible tool with which to get going, but the results can appear timid. Instead, a chunky graphite stick might enable you to make bolder, more immediate tonal drawings. Oil pastels are also perfect for drawing loose, gestured lines and can be overpainted with watercolor or leftover Jacquard Procion dyes for fabulous resist effects. Even experienced artists find it difficult to come up with ideas out of the blue, so don't even try; look to your inspirational sources for the answers. What colors are present in the things you have seen or collected? Are there patterns, repeated shapes, motifs, lines with which you can work?

Ideas Become Quilts

We invest a lot of time in our sketchbooks. We realize they are an invaluable part of the process of our quiltmaking. It's the place where we generate and develop ideas, audition color themes, and create designs. Sometimes the sketchbook will exist for a long time before any textile work will be generated from it, but more often than not, we'll be working toward an idea for a quilt from the beginning. It can seem like a giant leap from sketchbook page to wall quilt, but there are various ways in which you can make that transition easier.

Sampling

Laura likes to keep fabric samples alongside her artwork in the sketchbooks. By removing most of a page from the book and leaving just a flap of about 1½" (4 cm) at the spine, she can insert a replacement page of fabric. This fabric page might be just a bit of dyed fabric in the colors of the theme, or it may be a sample stitched to try out a technique she'll use later in the quilt. The joining of the new page can become part of the design, too. Perhaps it's attached with big, bold hand stitches using embroidery thread, or maybe shiny metallic thread sewn by machine. We often attach and insert extensions to pages using colorful metal eyelets or brads to add accents of color and make a real visual statement.

Stitching Your Sketchbook

Stitch can be used to embellish your sketchbook page, be it paper or fabric. Machine stitching can be fun and quick, but just remember to keep the stitch length a little longer than the default, or all of those perforations made by the needle will inevitably weaken the page and it may tear. To avoid this we sometimes reinforce the paper by first fusing it to lightweight interfacing or by sticking a second sheet of paper to the back of the page after the stitching is complete. Handstitching can be used to great effect, too. Keep the stitches simple for the best results. Try lines of horizontal bar stitches, big cross stitches, or maybe just a simple running stitch. Paper is much less flexible than fabric, so you'll need to take care not to rip the page as you draw the thread through.

Above all, we keep the step from sketchbook page to fabric very simple by using many of the same techniques. We paint and draw on paper, and we do the same on fabric. It's usually just a matter of switching watercolor or acrylic for dye or fabric paint. Paper collage is just the same as appliqué. The drawn line translates beautifully into the quilted or embroidered line. And as for all of that ephemera? If you want to include it in your textile work, just try one of the many digital image photo-transfer products, or simply sew it on directly for a paper-and-stitch mixed-media quilt.

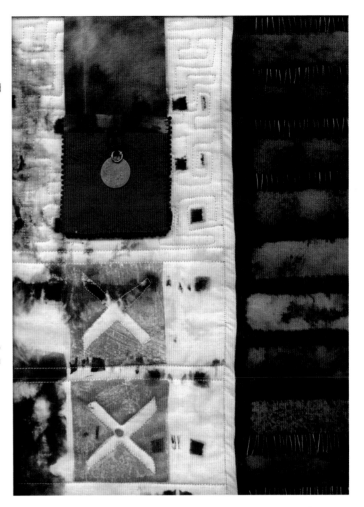

Detail of Linda's discharged and printed cotton and linen quilt, "Talisman," 25" W x 27½" L (64cm x 70cm).

Our sketchbooks are constantly a work in progress. We rarely get to the last page of a book before becoming inspired by a new theme or just being tempted to buy another new gorgeous sketchbook. Don't be overly cautious with your book, but if you treat it with care this thoughtfully created resource will last for a lifetime of quiltmaking. Keep adding to it when you find something relevant, and don't be afraid to work back into old pages with new ideas. As you evolve as a quilter, your sketchbooks can keep up with you, always providing a wealth of ideas and resources. We often like to look back through old sketchbooks that we haven't referred to for a while; we usually find little gems that we didn't pursue at the time but are now perfect for a new challenge.

Sketchbooks that are tended and nurtured, that are given their due respect, are almost always exquisite things, things you will want to cherish and value. For us, our sketchbooks are the most valuable resource of visual inspiration we have.

The "Big-Eared Bear" looks up from my sketchbook page with wonder in his expression, and I can see him wandering around a forest of poker-straight daisies. I found another page in my sketchbook that contained daisies and thought to combine the two to create a whimsical scene.

Sketchbook to Quilt

Melanie Testa

I HAVE SPENT MANY AN HOUR encamped in a favorite coffee shop with paint box, dropper bottle, pens, pencils, and white paint at the ready. This time is a retreat for me, an opportunity to disengage with daily life and begin to really look at what is around me. I can pick up my pencil, evaluate my surroundings, and draw.

Not every day is meant for detailed drawings. On those days, I know it is time to doodle, to give my imagination free rein and allow it to soar. I might lazily touch my paint-filled brush to the paper and see what happens, or draw a little illustration that has been floating in the back of my consciousness. Whatever happens when I open my sketchbook, I don't judge it; I keep doing it until I have page after page to draw upon in the making of an art quilt. This is what keeping an artist's journal is about for me: It is the ability to engage my creative mind outside my sewing room doors and think about the world and my surroundings in a new and different light. My sketchbook allows me to practice my drawing skills, work with color, and play with fresh ideas. There are times when I will re-create a page in my book as closely as I am able. Other times I will grab one motif from one page and another from another page and bring the two elements together. The great thing about journaling is that as you continue to work with it, you will find ways to meld the ideas created on paper into your art quilt.

Interpreting Sketchbook Imagery into Fabric

One idea you can try is to combine imagery from several different sketchbook pages into one piece of fabric. In the following example, I brought two ideas together from different pages and combined them into a 4" x 6" (10cm x 15cm) quilt.

"L'existence," 21" W x 44" L (53cm x 112cm).
This art quilt is the direct result of combining imagery from my sketchbook pages. I really love its complexity and wouldn't have been able to come up with this intricate design without the inspiration of my sketchbooks.

Technique to Try

Materials

- Sketchbook filled with images
- Tracing paper
- Mechanical pencil for tracing
- Materials for small quilt, including fabrics, batting, fusible webbing (Wonder-Under), sewing machine, threads, etc.

DIRECTIONS

STEP 1: Choose elements from various pages that you would like to combine into one piece of fiber art.

STEP 2: Create a map or pattern. I play with pattern and scale using a piece of tracing paper for each motif of my finished quilt. Tracing paper allows you to move the different layers around, erase pencil marks, and reposition motifs until you have the final composition of a piece nailed down.

STEP 3: Make registration marks (marks that delineate the motif field and help align all of the layers of paper when you are ready to check that the motif on each layer is correctly placed in relation to the others) on each layer of paper. Simply choose a size of rectangle or square that is larger than your largest motif, and make 4 marks on each piece of paper that defines the corners of your rectangle or square. If you are planning a finished piece as small as 4" x 6" (10 cm x 15 cm), the registration marks will reflect the outside edges of the quilt. Tape each of your layers down. This pattern or map can be used in a strict manner by placing your quilt under the pattern or it can be followed loosely. I usually follow patterns loosely, but I find that having a pattern can help me out of a tight spot quite nicely.

STEP 4: To prepare the background, cut the batting and backing so it is ¼" (.64 cm) larger than your finished piece will be.

STEP 5: Use your pattern to trace the motifs onto fabrics that you will fuse to your piece. You can eyeball the placement of your motifs by comparing it to your pattern or you can slide the fiber work under the tracing and use the pattern as a strict guide.

***

The background of "Big-Eared Bear" is actually two pieces of fabric; the top layer is a hand-dyed green China silk which nods colorwise at the original painting of the daisies. However, I also wanted to bring in the jagged line that surrounded the big-eared bear from the journal piece into the fiber-art interpretation, so I traced the jagged pattern piece, cut it out of a turquoise fabric, and placed that under the green silk. Admittedly, this is a vague addition to the composition as a whole, so I handstitched lines that end abruptly when they touch the jagged line. This becomes a horizon line that, by the nature of its height, serves to highlight the size of the bear in comparison to the daisies, drawing the eye upward.

The various sketchbook pages I chose to inspire my little quilt.

Here you see the quilt is coming together. My fabrics have been fused, the bear has been added, but it still feels a little bland and missing that something special.

Evaluate Your Design

At this point in the process, evaluate the design and composition to see if the piece is lacking. If it feels unfinished and needs more imagery, try leafing through your sketchbook pages to see if there are other motifs you could add to your piece. For this piece, I flipped through my journal pages and came across a small brown-and-peach-colored painting. This small painting has Os ascending to the upper right corner of the canvas. These O shapes tend to pop up in various guises throughout my journals, so I opted to add them to my little quilt using the same process that I employed to create the bear, with tracing paper and fusible webbing.

Embellishment

Now is the time to add any hand or machine stitching and embellishment to your piece. In this piece I hand embroidered the daisy stems and also stitched on sequins and beads.

Because of the fleeting nature of creativity, had I not gotten this big-eared bear down on paper, I might not have created this small work of art. Visual memory requires that we get the idea down on paper and outside of the confines of our minds. When you first start to record these thoughts and memories, your results may seem sophomoric and you may need to close your book and hide your efforts—even from yourself. I can assure you that after years of maintaining a visual diary, your efforts will become works of art themselves.

Journal quilting is a terrific means to practice design concepts, interpret images from your sketchbooks and photographs, audition a new idea for a series of quilts, and hone quilting skills. By committing to make a small quilt every week for one year, your quilting and creative skills will increase dramatically.

~tip~

❧ To create the bear, I used the original painting in my sketchbook as a guide, tracing the bear onto tracing paper. I then laid a small piece of white cloth over this pattern and traced the bear onto the cloth using a mechanical pencil, creating a sharp, thin line. I shaded the bear's belly, ears, eyes, and nose with gray paint. I applied fusible webbing to the back, carefully cut on the penciled outline, then removed the backing and attached the bear with an iron.

Above left: Wool fabric; freehand machine embroidered with rayon embroidery thread and rubbed with Shiva Paintstiks. Above right: Upholstery fabric, synthetic gold organza; drawn with Neocolor water-soluble crayons, handstitched with cotton variegated thread, and punch-needle embroidered.

Eco-Friendly Journal Quilting Techniques
Natalya Aikens

INSPIRED BY QUILT ARTIST JEANNE WILLIAMSON and her weekly journal quilts, I challenged myself to create a small artwork once a week for a year. For 2007, my goal was to make 5" x 5" (18cm x 18cm) weekly quilts with recycled items. My goal for a long time has been to make recycled materials look beautiful.

I have always been interested in eco-consciousness. Back in my fashion design days, I read up on the ecologically correct production of fabric, the recycling of fabric waste, and designing garments from organically grown cotton or hemp and recycled fabrics. A friend of mine and I actually sat down and researched the possibility of such a design firm, came up with a business plan and … nothing happened… Lack of funds was the main reason for our idea not coming to fruition, followed closely by the overwhelming amount of work it would entail.

Fast-forward to a few years ago—the fashion career is long gone; the costume career is on hold; child rearing is at the forefront. I needed a creative outlet. I started making baby quilts and, remembering that I had made some art quilts years earlier, wanted to make some again. A new creative urge was released, but another feeling started creeping in—all of this waste, the scraps left over, the new fabric I wanted to buy, all the new toys, er, tools I needed … it just felt wrong. So I started collecting my scraps and curbed the urge to buy new fabric for every new project. Then I found my old file of ideas and research from that fashion eco-project all those lifetimes ago, and I saw the samples of fabrics I had made using plastic bags and junk-food wrappers; it was a lightbulb moment! I can use all of this in my art. I remembered struggling with how to make the recycled materials beautiful enough to want to wear them and realized that this task might be easier with non-wearable art, as the end product doesn't have to be comfortable.

Making one quilt a week for a year can seem like a daunting task. The following are some guidelines I came up with to help you accomplish this goal. And remember—these are small quilts!

Do not stress over this project. This is a very important rule; life in general is stressful enough, so do whatever you can each week. This will help to keep the process of making art enjoyable. Some weeks are too busy for intellectual or elaborate art, so just make something easy. Try using a scrap of painted fabric and do some free-motion machine embroidery over it, with no particular pattern in mind. Or just fuse some contrasting or complementary scraps together and stitch a few interesting stitches on them. The point is to carve out time every week to create art consistently.

Stick to a small size for your quilt. Small projects are easier to complete, and they are less stressful. I happened to find a small photo album on sale, so I chose 5" x 5" (18cm x 18cm) as the size for my quilts so I could store them in the album.

Time is a flexible notion. If you don't complete a weekly quilt in one week's time, don't stress about it and give up. In my mind, a week is Monday through Sunday; that's how it's done in Russia and I haven't retrained myself in twenty-eight years, so it won't happen now. But if it's Monday and last week's quilt isn't done yet, it's okay. And I can even take until Tuesday or Wednesday to get it done. Knowing that it's okay if it isn't done will keep me going in this project so I don't quit altogether.

Be creative in choosing recycled materials for your quilts. Sometimes I'll use a plastic bag or sometimes I'll choose scraps from a previous project. Try dryer lint as batting and choose alternate backing fabrics; no one will see them. As long as something is recycled, you have fulfilled your mission. And if you have managed to make something recycled look beautiful, it's a bonus!

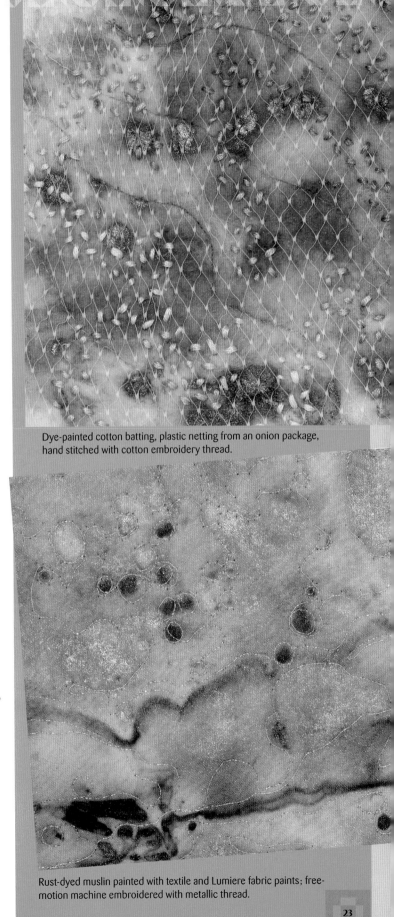

Dye-painted cotton batting, plastic netting from an onion package, hand stitched with cotton embroidery thread.

Rust-dyed muslin painted with textile and Lumiere fabric paints; free-motion machine embroidered with metallic thread.

Detail of handpainted muslin; dry grass, leaves, and bark coated with Mod Podge, glued, and handstitched with thick silk thread.

Ideas for Recycled Materials

- Use plastics. Crumple, heat, color, and stitch plastic materials you see every day, such as grocery and produce bags.

- Think of dryer lint as art material. I collect the lint from my dryer after it's done with my girls' sweaters. I never even knew the bonus I would receive when I bought them brightly colored sweaters in different fuzzy yarns—they produce such colorful lint! I trap the lint between layers of sheer netting, organza, or chiffon. You can handstitch it, free-motion stitch it, and even drip paint and dye over it. Also try used dryer sheets as backing fabric for your quilts. And as a bonus, if you used the scented ones, your journal quilt smells like fresh laundry!

- Take the waste backing paper from adhesive shipping labels and see what they look like after you crumple, wet, and then paint them.

- Don't throw giftwrap tissue away. I rip tissue papers in small pieces and trap them between scraps of shiny synthetic organza and practice different hand stitches around them. I draw and paint on wrapping tissue and then see how it holds up to machine stitching—very well indeed.

- Save envelopes from overseas mail bearing all the different stamps and markings. Put Mod Podge or a light coat of gel medium over the stamps, allow it to dry, and then stitch the stamps onto fabric.

- Save ticket stubs from buses and museums to make a collage with fabric scraps and stitching.

- Use papers with printer errors. When my printer begins to run out of ink while printing, sometimes I end up with sheets of illegible pages. Apply matte gel medium to these papers and stitch them to fabric for interesting patterns.

- A package arrives with something wrapped in white perforated paper for protection, and guess what? That paper looks good painted and trapped between sheer netting.

- Use and stitch paper towels that have been used to clean up painting projects. Oftentimes, colorful combinations will appear on paper towels when you're cleaning up after a project.

- Look at everyday objects as embellishments for your quilts. Found objects have always piqued my interest. I just could not throw away the tiny glass tiles from a rejected sample for our bathroom remodel. And now they are glued and stitched in a journal quilt. My kids collected bark and leaves on a walk; I put gel medium on them and stitched them to scraps of fabric and made a little nature collage.

- Use your journal quilts to experiment with designs and techniques for larger pieces. After experimenting with techniques in a smaller format, you'll have a better sense of what will work for larger bodies of work.

Use this quilt journaling as an exercise to help find your creative voice. I work intuitively most of the time. Sometimes there is deep thought behind the art, especially when I am working from a specific inspiration for a bigger piece. Sometimes I literally throw things down and my eye notices an exciting element and I go from there. These small works of art are tools to train both your eye and your thought process to be able to focus better, and also to train yourself to listen to your intuition with an open mind.

Stay committed. During my first week's quilt I was feeling very hopeful about this project for the new year. I was excited about that first weekly quilt: the pretty pink plastic bag, the white feather that my youngest pulled out of her pillow, brightly colored threads captured on the bag, a scrap of sheer white organza finished off with blanket stitching in silk and rayon threads, and a bit of glamour with a few glass beads. These are just going to be beautiful, I thought to myself, but I was quickly stumped by week two.

Realize that it may take a while to get into the rhythm. Some weeks you may find your head is brimming with ideas to use in your weekly journal quilt, so much so that you don't know which idea to use. Tip: Write your ideas down so you can use them in future quilts.

Think of this endeavor as your own private "Project Runway" challenge. Perhaps you've got an hour right now; make a piece of art. Make it work!

Finishing Your Quilts

Use these weekly quilts as an opportunity to play with different edges and finishes.

✳ Decorative stitching
You could do a study in the blanket stitch (for example) by stitching with different thread weights or using different spacing patterns between each stitch for an organic effect. Or you could sew several laps of straight stitching around the perimeter.

✳ Glues and adhesives
Glue the edges together and then paint them with acrylic paint.

✳ Acrylic or fabric paint
Simply paint the edges with a foam brush. If the batting starts getting fuzzy because of the paint, tease it out some more and go for that hairy look.

✳ Frayed edge
Unravel a few threads from the ends, and now you have a raw edge that adds more texture to your quilt.

In the next chapter, we'll begin to explore texture, the use of color, and proportion, and learn how you do not need to be formally trained in the principles of design to create incredible art quilts.

Detail of "Derevnya: Russian Fairytale Village 2," 59" W x 48" L (150cm x 122cm).

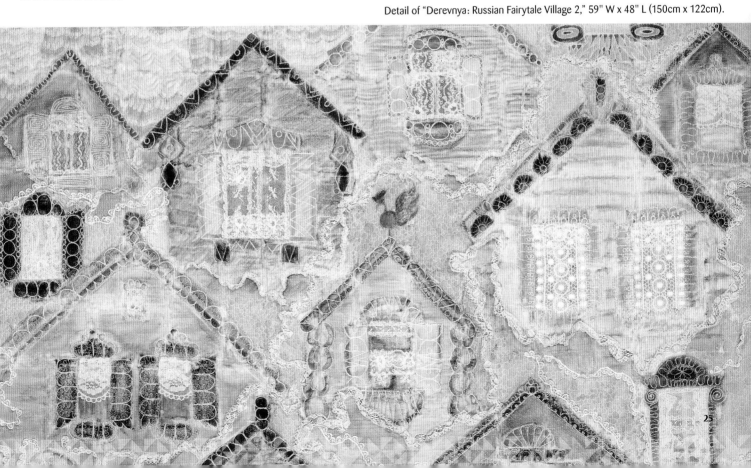

Chapter Two
ART & DESIGN PRINCIPLES

Lyric Kinard

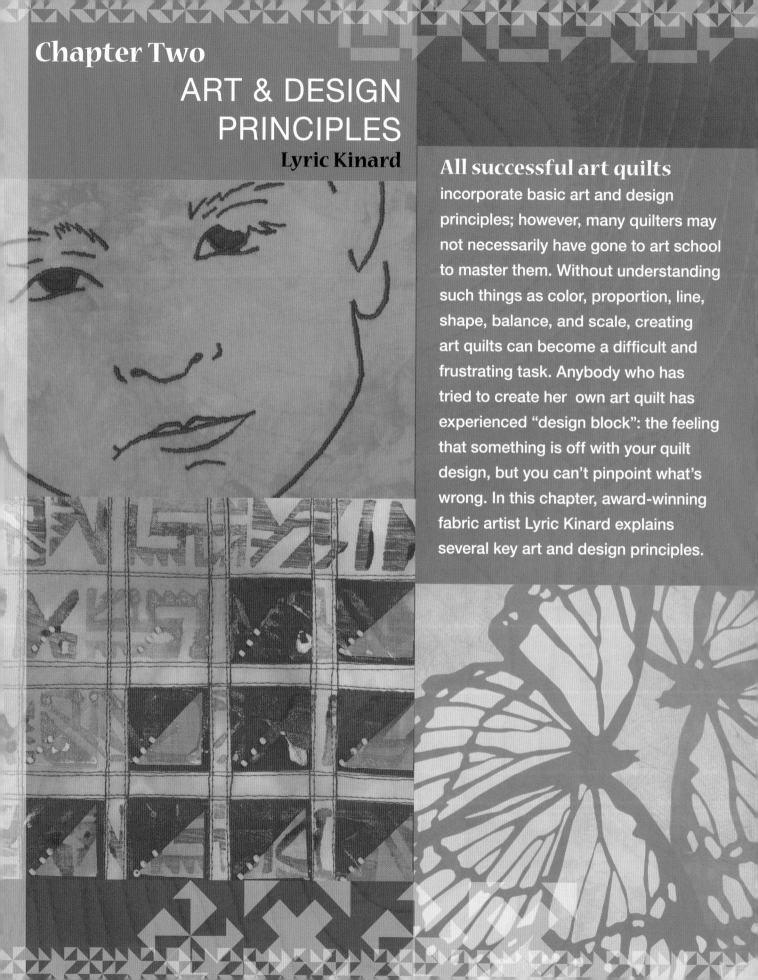

All successful art quilts incorporate basic art and design principles; however, many quilters may not necessarily have gone to art school to master them. Without understanding such things as color, proportion, line, shape, balance, and scale, creating art quilts can become a difficult and frustrating task. Anybody who has tried to create her own art quilt has experienced "design block": the feeling that something is off with your quilt design, but you can't pinpoint what's wrong. In this chapter, award-winning fabric artist Lyric Kinard explains several key art and design principles.

"Three Leaves," 22" W x 18" L (56cm x 46cm).

Unity and Focal Point

I CAN'T COUNT THE NUMBER of times people have looked at my work then wistfully said to me, "I wish I were creative or artistic." When that happens, I just take a deep breath, smile, and launch into my favorite soapbox speech: I firmly believe that everyone is creative in some way and that being an artist is something we can all learn. Why do people think that artists are just born, springing like Athena from the head of Zeus, fully formed and ready to go?

Do we hand a five-year-old the works of Shakespeare and, when she can't understand them, say, "Well, you're just not a reader"? No! We teach her letters and the sounds they make. We teach her to put those letters together to make words, and then she practices and progresses until many years later she can pick up a Shakespeare play and not only make sense of it, but enjoy it. She might even go on to write sonnets or a play herself.

In the same way you learn your alphabet and eventually learn to read, you can learn the fundamental principles of art. These basic building blocks help you to better understand, interpret, and enjoy the world of art. They will help you to get that creative vision out of your head and onto canvas, paper, or fabric. You might have already mastered many sewing and quilting techniques, but I liken that to having perfect penmanship without knowing how to read. Mastering the elements of art is like learning to write poetry with that perfect penmanship. Forget that unfortunate incident in second grade when an unkind comment convinced you that you weren't an artist. It's never too late to learn your alphabet, put together words, and practice until you, too, can write poetry with your needle and thread. Here I present basic art-design principles to help you on your fiber art journey.

Example A.

Example B.

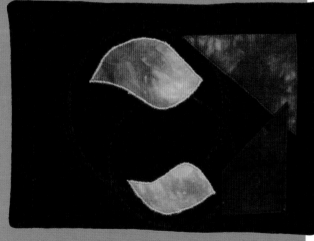

Example C.

Unity

When you look at any work of art, your eye sees it first as a whole, not as a lot of separate parts. Unity means that all the parts visually fit together, that nothing jangles your nerves unless the artist intends it to. Harmony and consistency are good words to describe unity. If Romeo appeared at Juliet's balcony and said, "O speak again bright angel for thou art a wicked-hot babe," it just wouldn't sound right, would it? Much modern slang clashes with Elizabethan English. Artists, too, strive for a consistent style.

PROXIMITY

One of the easiest ways to achieve unity in a work of art is through proximity. Letters in proximity to one another create words. Words grouped together create sentences that convey meaning. Sometimes poets even place their words in groups that mean as much visually as intellectually.

Look at example A. These random shapes scattered on a background really don't mean anything or read as a visual whole. You could scatter various pieces of fabric, beads, and assorted embellishments all over a gorgeous background, but the separate elements don't really create a unified composition unless you are purposely going for the Jackson Pollock effect. His compositions were unified in their technique, but random variety—bordering on chaos—was the name of the game for him. When you take those same shapes and place them in proximity to one another, they read as a visual whole (example B). They look more like a sentence than alphabet pasta floating in your soup. Most viewers see them as more interesting and can read some meaning into the work as a whole.

REPETITION

Another way to achieve unity in artwork is through repetition. When words repeat a pattern of syllables or sounds, they create a pleasing rhythm, becoming poetry or music lyrics. Most quilt makers are familiar with repetition as a design element because the basic traditional quilt form is repeated blocks in a grid pattern. Repeating shape, color, or direction of lines (among many other things) can serve to unify a visual work. In example B there is a repetition of diagonal lines and triangular shapes that unifies the composition. Colors in the warm red to yellow range are also repeated. But if a round, turquoise element were thrown in, it would stop the eye and catch your attention whether you wanted it to or not.

CONTINUATION

Continuation, a third way to achieve unity, is subtler than proximity or repetition. Continuing a line, shape, or color allows the eye to flow easily from one element to the next. In example C the eye follows the diagonal center edge up to the curved edge of the orange bit. The red quilted lines hold you for just a second, then bring you around again to where you started.

Focal Point

A billboard or magazine advertisement has a second or two to capture your attention; you should immediately understand what is being advertised, or it is virtually useless. In visual art this main idea is called the focal point. An artist uses various devices to draw your eye to the main idea of her piece and hold you there for a second or two before you take in the other supporting details. When creating your art, ask yourself if you want to emphasize something and how much you want to emphasize it. Remember that a focal point needs to be harmonious with the overall design and also realize that you can choose not to have a focal point if you wish. Traditional quilts with repetitive blocks or Andy Warhol's paintings of soup cans do very well without focal points. A poet chooses to use capitalization, rhyme, or punctuation only as it serves her purpose.

ISOLATION

One way to create this main idea of a focal point is through isolation. Placing one element apart from all of the others will draw your attention to it, as in example D. One block tumbling out of the stack will be noticed; one person standing apart from the crowd draws your attention.

PLACEMENT

Another device artists use to create a focal point is placement. Any element placed in the center of a symmetrical design will draw your attention like a bull's-eye. You can also put an element where lines point to it, as demonstrated in both examples D and E. Many architectural scenes or landscapes will have perspective lines leading to a vanishing point. The lines moving your eye to the focal point can be as subtle as the curve of an arm or as obvious as the center of a spiral. We humans are also programmed to follow the gaze of another, so if people in an artwork are all looking at something, it will become a focal point.

CONTRAST

Using contrast in an artwork is another way to create a focal point. Place a vertical element among many horizontal elements, an open space among many objects, a realistic image among abstract designs, a detailed section amid plainness, or a large element among many smaller ones. All of these techniques will draw your attention to the element that contrasts with everything around it. Example E has a round orange object surrounded by straight lines and darker purples. It is left unstitched, while the rest of the piece is quilted. Anything that contrasts in this way with its surroundings will stand out and become a focal point.

Example D.

Example E.

Techniques to Try

- ▣ Create a unified composition by repeating shape or color.
- ▣ Create a unified composition with mostly horizontal or vertical lines.
- ▣ Create one composition emphasizing unity, another emphasizing variety.
- ▣ Using five random shapes, create unity through proximity.
- ▣ Create a focal point using contrast of color, line, or detail.
- ▣ Create a focal point contrasting realistic/abstract, open/complex, size, or detail.
- ▣ Create a focal point using placement.
- ▣ Create a focal point using isolation.

✳✳✳

Remind yourself that learning to write verse like Shakespeare takes practice. Grab a friend or two and take some time to play around. Have fun, learn something new, make bad art, and learn from your failures. Give up the need to create a masterpiece every time you touch fabric. Remember, Athena was born a goddess, but we mere mortals must learn our craft one step at a time.

Color relationships: primary, secondary, and tertiary colors.

The Color Wheel

FOR MANY OF US, CHOOSING WHICH COLOR to use and where to place it in our artwork is strictly intuitive. We know which colors we like to work with, and use those same combinations over and over. We've also probably experienced that frustrating moment when we know a fabric just isn't working but have no idea what to do about it. Taking a little time and effort to learn some basic color theory will help you overcome that hurdle and understand more clearly what you are doing. Your art will become richer and more satisfying when you have an expanded palette with which to create.

Look at your most recent creation. Are the colors in your quilt "acting" in a well-rehearsed ensemble, or is a badly behaved diva stealing the show? Does the supporting cast help your star shine or are they bringing out the yawns? The first thing we must understand is that color is all about relationships. Not only do we all have an emotional relationship with color, but colors often interact with each other in interesting and unexpected ways. Think of colors as a troupe of actors on a stage. An actress might not change her looks, but she can elicit many different reactions from an audience depending on the part she plays and how she interacts with the rest of the troupe. She might be part of the chorus in one play and the star in the next. Similarly, a red apple might not stand out much in a bowl full of other red apples, but place it in a pile of fish and it becomes the center of attention.

Colors as Actors

Colors play on our emotions just like players on the stage. An actor can make us laugh in one scene and cry in the next without ever changing his costume. Consider for a moment the emotional way we use color in our language. We "see red," "feel blue," are "green with envy," have a bit of a "yellow streak," or are in a "black mood." Blue can evoke the feeling of tranquil waters, a crisp spring sky, or the grayed shadow of depression. A landscape that is predominantly blue might feel calm and serene while the same scene in a series of reds is going to be much more dynamic. Reds are very active and can evoke feelings of passion, danger, or welcome. The red of a child's toy ball feels joyful while the same color evokes danger and fear when depicting a pool of blood. All of these emotional relationships to individual colors can be used intentionally in our artwork to make a greater impact on the viewer.

We all have personal preferences, and emotions linked to color can also be very individual. Take a good look at your stash and you will probably find a definite lack of orange if that is your least favorite color. Where does your prejudice come from? Did the hated rival team that clobbered you in the championship game your senior year wear orange? Conversely, is your stash loaded with blues that you just simply couldn't pass by? Guess what? You can make that gorgeous bright blue go from being merely your favorite fabric to one that sings right out loud if you place it next to a little deep, rusty orange. It's all about how the two colors relate to each other.

Notice how the warm colors move forward and the cool grays and blues recede.

The cool blues in this piece create a restful feeling.

Color Relationships

Just as most plays need a whole cast of characters, colors in our artwork seldom work alone. Let's look at a basic twelve-step color wheel and learn how colors relate to each other. The three colors that we start with are the primary colors of red, yellow, and blue. A printer might use magenta, yellow, and cyan and the dye artist burgundy, gold, and navy, but they are still the primary red, yellow, and blue from which all the other colors are mixed. They are the main characters that the director casts first and then fills in the supporting roles around them. When the three primaries are onstage at the same time it is called a triadic color scheme. Each attracts a lot of attention and things are usually pretty lively. Any three colors that form an equilateral triangle on the wheel also form a triadic color scheme when used together as the main colors in a piece of art.

The next three colors on the wheel are the secondary colors: green, orange, and purple, each being an equal mixture of two primaries. The six tertiary colors are mixtures of a primary and whatever secondary is next to it on the color wheel, such as yellow-orange, blue-green, and so on. These supporting actors add depth and interest to the piece. When one actor is speaking alone onstage it is called a monologue.

When only one color is used in art it is called a monochromatic color scheme. You may use orange in a range of deep rust to pale peach, but it's still just one color on the color wheel taking center stage. Conversely, when actors sing together in a chorus, they all have slightly different voices but together they sound similar. Like-wise, when all of the colors in an artwork are next to each other on the color wheel it is called an analogous color scheme. It could be yellow all the way to red or turquoise through blue-violet, but the colors are all similar and don't usually compete for attention. An artwork made with analogous colors is usually calmer than, say, one with a triadic color scheme.

Action on the stage creates excitement, and the strong contrast between red and green or red, orange, and turquoise has the same effect. The colors opposite each other on the color wheel are called complementary colors, and using them as dominant players can achieve a glowing luminosity or even a subtle vibra-tion. Each of these color schemes can be used to your advantage as an artist. Do you want one color to pop? Place it next to its complement. Want a subtler effect? Try an analogous scheme. The relationships the colors have to each other are more important than the colors themselves.

Value

An actress can have quite a different impact depending on whether she is in the center of a bright spotlight or lurking in the shadows—the same thing happens with color. The amount of light a color is given is called its value. The palest blue has a very high-value tint. A very deep, low-value, almost midnight blue-black is called a shade. A tint is a color mixed with white, while a shade is mixed with black.

The warm reds in this piece create an active feeling.

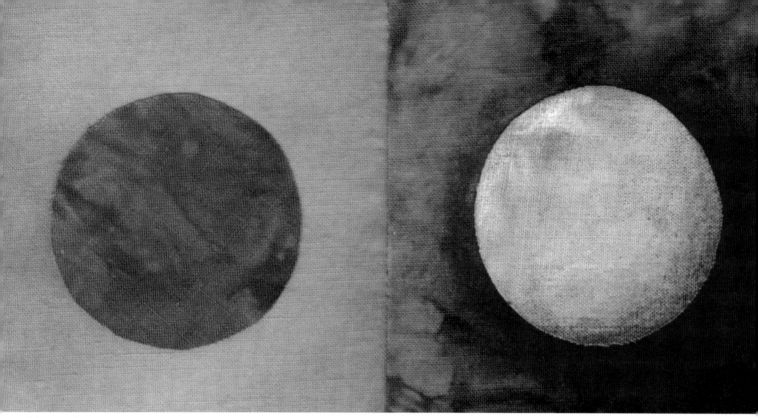

Color vs. value.

When an artist is creating, value is often more critical to the success of the piece than color. A turquoise and an orange of the same value placed next to each other will naturally create excitement, but a very dark, low-value turquoise will make a light, high-value orange seem to jump right off of the wall. Many times when a swatch of fabric just isn't working in a piece it isn't because of its color, it is because it is the wrong value of that color. If you have access to a digital camera, take a picture of your artwork in black and white. If one of the fabrics seems too dark or too light for the rest of the composition, this will quickly show you if one of your fabrics is the wrong value. You can also view your piece through a red plastic report cover to analyze its value. Look to see if you have created an unintentional focal point with a dark or light value fabric or embellishment.

The value of the colors in your artwork can create specific effects such as the illusion of distance. Something depicted with high-value contrast will appear to come forward while a low-value contrast will appear to recede. Warm colors such as red and orange also appear to come forward while cool colors seem to move away. Objects seen from a distance will appear grayer and bluer, as in the smoky purple of distant mountains. Volume and depth can also be created with the shading of one color from dark to light. The change in value alone turns a flat circle into a sphere.

Just as highly contrasting complementary colors create excitement, dramatic contrasts in value alone will be very dynamic. Low-value contrast in your art will be more understated and restrained.

Techniques to Try

- Make a monochromatic portrait or a landscape with a triadic color scheme.
- Create emotional pieces expressing joy or discord through the use of color alone.
- Assuming your stash is minimally organized (a big assumption, I know), sit down with the color wheel and make note of which colors you are missing. Even if your fabric is in one big pile on the floor, it will be fun to fondle and sort. Do you have a full range of values for each color? No? Great excuse for a trip to the fabric shop!

✳✳✳

Example A.

Texture, Shape, and Line

IN MOST ART TUTORIALS the element of line comes first, followed by shape, and then texture. This makes perfect sense, as our first artistic creation as children is usually a line made with the point of a pencil or crayon. That line then bends and meets itself to form a shape. Later we become aware of texture and work to add just the right patterns and details that will bring our artwork to life. As artists working with cloth, we journey in the opposite direction, choosing the texture of our fabric then cutting shapes and stitching lines. The wonderful thing about quilts as a medium is that each of these elements performs multiple tasks; line becomes texture, and texture becomes shape. Recognizing the unique way textile artists use texture, shape, and line will help us to more ably and effectively achieve our visions and connect with the viewer.

Texture

Texture is defined as the visual and tactile quality of a surface, or the way it feels when you touch it. Most art, however, is a cerebral rather than a physical, tactile experience. Our bodies want to participate, but it's not acceptable to reach out to touch a sculpture at a museum, sing out loud at the symphony, or leap out of your seat at the ballet. This desire to become involved in what we are experiencing is one of the ways the artist connects with the viewer, relying on the recollection of shared experiences to convey a message. We must have some knowledge of the ocean in order to understand an image of it. Painters must work hard to imitate texture, but we as textile artists have an advantage. We are aware of the feel of cloth from the time we are born and wrapped in our first blanket. It is our daily, intimate connection with fabric that allows textile art to evoke such an immediate response.

The very first step in our creative process is to determine the tactile quality of the surface of our work. It is the most physical connection between the viewer and the artwork. We can understand the work through touch, even with our eyes closed. The texture of cloth comes from both the fiber content and the weave. Look at example A. We know the feel of the smooth satin edge and the bumpiness of the beads and probably hold the memory of cotton sateen in our fingertips.

When coming from a quilting rather than a fine arts background, we often limit ourselves to plainly woven cotton. It is, after all, the standard material used for piecing and appliqué and we know how it behaves. Perhaps we should consider what effects different fibers and weaves might create. The long, lustrous fibers of silk will reflect light and present a very smooth surface, while velvet will absorb light and add a dimensional quality that is almost impossible for the fingers to resist. Think for a moment of how wools can be steamed into three-dimensional curves and perhaps new and interesting ideas will come to mind. Wool also brings to mind many different memories of touch such as warmth, softness, or itchiness. How can we as artists use those tactile associations to communicate with the viewer? Using these fibers might require variations from traditional quilting methods, but an expanded toolbox of techniques is never a bad thing.

Along with the fiber and weave, we also choose the cloth's visual texture. A brightly colored, bold floral print will have an entirely different visual texture than a homey brown plaid. Look at example B and compare it to example A. Both are hand-dyed cottons, but one is almost a solid color and the other is greatly varied, both in tactile and visual texture. Compare example B to example C. While both have very similar compositions and use the same kind of cloth the visual texture of each is quite different. Although example B is similar in composition to example C, I believe example C is a more interesting piece of art. The crackled texture of the hand-

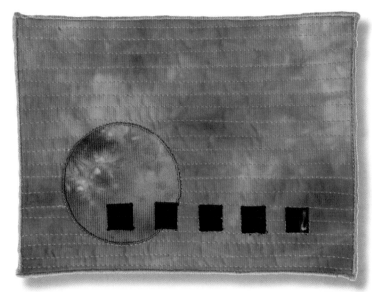

Example B (above) and Example C (below).

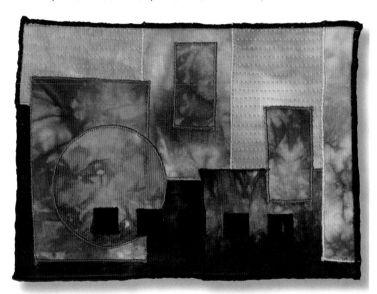

The hand-dyed fabrics in Example C add depth; the varied rectangles add interest and give the circle and squares context.

dyed fabric adds depth, the subtle shifts in background color and the varied rectangles add interest and give the circle and squares more context in which to exist, rather than just being shapes floating in space.

Shape

Once we have chosen our palette of cloth, we usually pick up the scissors and cut out shapes. Often the shape is part of a larger abstract pattern (such as a pieced quilt) or part of a larger pictorial object. Remember that the space around the object is a shape as well. Many times we become so focused on the main object we are creating, we end up just plopping it onto a background without

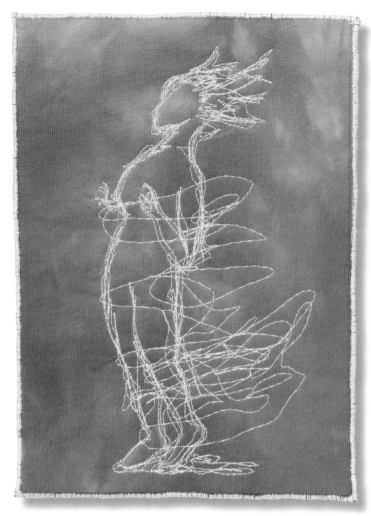

Example D is composed entirely of lines; their frenetic quality connotes motion and a sense of anxiety.

Example E is also composed entirely of lines but adds the elements of shape and texture.

thinking about the composition of the negative space. Would your piece be more interesting if the main object was integrated into the background? Take another look at examples B and C and decide for yourself.

Even when we are creating a purely abstract piece in which shapes don't represent any object, we humans can't help but assign meaning to those shapes. Ask viewers what they see when they look at abstract shapes in art and each person will say a different thing: a square becomes a box or a house, a circle becomes an apple, a moon, or a face. Look at example B for a minute and very quickly your brain will start making connections to the world around you. We should keep this in mind as we try to create a connection with the viewer.

Line

As the composition nears completion, we thread a needle and begin to work with line. Quilting is simply drawing with a needle and thread, another of the unique and exciting aspects of our medium. We have the option of an intermittent handstitch or a solid machine line. We can choose from unlimited colors, weights, and textures, and our stitches can outline, overlay, echo, or meander. Quilting lines can take a different direction from the composition of the top or emphasize each shape and add interest and texture to the negative space. Line can move the eye from one place to the other and can help create a focal point. Don't forget that each stitch will add to or detract from the overall composition. Quilted lines also do double duty as an added element of texture. If we use a heavy and contrasting colored thread, our line moves up the ladder of visual and tactile importance. If we use a blending color and a lighter-weight thread, our quilting lines disappear and the shadow made by the dip and valley of the batting lends subtle texture. Seed stitches can become crosshatching and varying thread colors change the value and add depth to a piece.

Look at examples D and E. Each composition relies primarily on line and uses the same kind of thread, but to different effects. The line in D is frenetic, unsure, and implies motion, while the line in E is sure, smooth, and bold. One feels anxious, while the other feels calm. Example F is also composed entirely of line but adds the elements of shape and texture. The shadows created by the thread dipping into the batting produce a visual texture, while the dimensional line of the embroidery evokes a tactile memory and boldly leads the eye around the piece. The heavy yellow line closing in on itself creates a shape and also becomes a focal point.

The lines in Example F are sure, smooth, and bold, evoking a feeling of calm.

Quilt artists also love to embellish their work with everything from fuzzy yarns to endless beads and doodads. Remember that each item added to our art should have a purpose in the composition. Each bead, bangle, or layer of burned-out organza will play a role as added texture, shape, and perhaps even line, and should be in harmony with the overall composition. In example A, the tiny beads march in a straight line, echoing the edges of the gold squares and the overall shape of the piece. If the beads were simply scattered on the surface, they would detract from the composition.

I encourage you to think more carefully about texture, shape, and line in your artwork. Look at art around you and analyze how these elements are used by other artists.

Techniques to Try

DIRECTIONS

◼ Use a different type of fiber or weave than your usual cloth. What technical challenges does this material present? How does the different texture affect the outcome of your piece?

◼ Create depth, motion, or a focal point using a visually patterned cloth that is different from that with which you are most comfortable.

◼ Create an abstract composition with shape, integrating the shapes into the background.

◼ Create another abstract shape composition, but this time pay more attention to the negative space (background) than the positive space (foreground).

◼ Create two compositions using line and shape: one still, one active. What is the dominant direction of line in each composition?

◼ Create a composition using line alone. Play with the weight and texture of your line. What emotions can you evoke with line alone?

Emily Parson's 58"x 58" (147cm x 147cm) quilt "Mariposas" makes a big impact from afar, whereas Janet Lasher's 1" (3cm) beaded brooch (inset) requires intimacy.

Scale, Proportion, and Balance

THERE ARE MANY DIFFERENT WAYS to communicate with visual art. Sometimes you want to make sure that everyone in the world hears what you have to say, but other times you might wish to whisper a hint into one ear alone. When you learn about the elements of scale and proportion in art, you are learning about the kind of connection you want to make with your audience. This doesn't mean that something has to be overwhelmingly large to have a great impact. On a stage full of musicians, a soloist is able to command the attention of an audience with a few simple tricks. Learning those tricks, such as how to balance the elements within your artwork, will help you to communicate your vision clearly, whether you whisper or shout it out loud.

Scale

Just as a musician knows how to play differently for each venue, an artist must be aware of how her work will relate to the viewer in different contexts. The volume of a musician's sound is like the scale of an artist's work. The bigger the theater, the bigger the sound. The scale of a work of art in relation to the viewer, its human scale, is often the first consideration an artist makes when taking a commission. Is the artwork going to be displayed high up on the atrium wall of a large business complex or will it hang by the front door in a private home? Public spaces often call for large-scale works and will be able to have an impact on many viewers at once.

Take a look at Emily Parson's beautiful quilt "Mariposas." It has a strong and immediate impact even from a distance and can be admired by many people at once. Its large size is like the amplifier that allows thousands to hear a band simultaneously. The context of the subject's scale within an artwork will also have a great effect. Magnifying something that is usually quite small can capture your attention through sheer surprise. A butterfly wing that fills your entire field of vision gains significance as you see the extraordinary details that are seldom noticed in everyday life. We are all familiar with Georgia O'Keeffe's enlargements of flowers, imbuing nature's little wonders with a grandeur that was seldom seen before the artist's time.

A small-scale artwork, on the other hand, will speak to one person at a time, often drawing her physically closer in an intimate exchange of ideas. The impact of the work can be no less enthralling than a large-scale work, just as a whisper can have as much meaning as a shout. Janet Lasher's tiny treasure of a beaded brooch is almost too small to be appreciated from more than a few feet away. Its intimate scale invites the viewer to come closer and discover its beauty one bead at a time. It is like six guitar strings intricately plucked for your ears alone. Both of these artworks make an effective connection to the viewer through the use of scale.

Proportion

Scale can also refer to the subject within the frame or its internal proportions. Proportion refers to either the size of the work in relation to something else or the way the size of the elements within a work of art relate to each other.

A soloist is given greater importance than the rest of the band by turning a spotlight on her, or just by having her step forward from the group. The larger the scale of any one element within an artwork, the greater its emphasis. Artists have often used exaggerated scale in religious artwork, making the main figure larger to enhance its importance. Advertisers also often use exaggerated proportions to emphasize their product. Take a look at advertisements around you and try to analyze what techniques are used to capture your attention so that you can use them when your visual message needs a little amplification. A contrast of scale can also be used to achieve interesting effects.

The proportions of elements in relation to one another can also imply depth and space. Larger elements will appear to come forward, and the same elements shown in a smaller size will appear to recede. The face on the right side in "On Stage" is shown at a vastly larger scale than the violinist onstage who appears to be some distance away. The close-up internal scale used for "Haven" achieves a completely different effect even though the subject is similar. Although the works are roughly the same size, their differing internal proportions convey different messages to the viewer. That large screen at the amphitheater can show you the entire band or give you a close-up of the guitar player's fast and furious fretwork.

"On Stage," 9¾" x 9¾" (25cm x 25cm). The face on the right side appears to come forward, while the person on the left appears to recede because of the figures' contrasting scales.

"Haven,"
17¾" W x 14¾" L
(45cm x 38cm).
Close-up internal
proportions create
a different effect for
the viewer.

Balance

Moving on to the element of balance, let's imagine the rock band again. That screaming electric guitar solo is astounding, but if that wild abandon was sustained throughout the concert, many a lovely ballad would be ruined. Fortunately, the musician has a volume control and has learned the concept of balance. The concept of balance is as tricky for a musician as it is for an artist. It is an element that is almost unnoticeable except when things aren't working in a piece. When a musical group is out of balance, such as that one soprano who refuses to "blend" in the community choir, the results are painfully obvious.

There are many different kinds of balance. Because of gravity, we expect the greatest visual weight to be at the bottom of a work of art. Usually the largest element or the darkest color lies near the bottom of the artwork, lending an appearance of stability and calm. Moving the visual weight away from the lower part of the artwork can create imbalance, give the effect of transition, of impending motion, or even of danger.

Symmetrical balance, often called "formal" balance, arranges the elements within a work of art equally on either side of a central vertical axis. This kind of balance is often static and quiet and can be quite dignified. Look at much of the architecture around you and you will find a stately, symmetrical balance. Traditional quilts often make use of symmetrical balance. Crystallographic balance gives equal emphasis to each part of the work, such as in most repeated block patterns. Or think of a perfectly blended choir where no one voice can be heard above another. Radial balance is used for Hawaiian appliqué or mariner's compass quilts, where elements radiate from a center like a bull's-eye.

Elements within a piece of art can vary quite a bit from each other but still receive equal visual weight. A small area of bright color can balance a larger, plain area just as a small, complex shape or textured element can balance a larger, plain element. The lead singer in a band will often wear a flashy color while the rest of the band is more subdued. She will have as much visual weight as the rest of the band combined.

When thinking about balance, look at the designed world around you and learn to ask yourself how the artist achieved her compositional success. Where does the visual weight of the artwork lie? Is the artwork balanced symmetrically or asymmetrically? What other elements of art (color, value, texture, shape, line, focal point, scale, unity) are used to create a balanced composition? What is the scale of the work in relation to the viewer and is it appropriate? What is the internal scale of the artwork? How is proportion used within the artwork to achieve effects such as implied depth?

Just as a guitarist knows how to amplify sound to fill different venues, we as artists need to be aware of how scale affects the impact of our artwork on the viewer. Do we want to draw in viewers and capture their attention in a subtle way or do we want to shout out our ideas? Do we want to achieve a calm, quietly balanced piece, or do we want to spotlight one element like the soloist in a band? In your next artwork, pay attention to the use of scale, proportion, and balance and see if you can affect your viewer as well as a versatile musician plays to her audience.

"Balance 2," 4" W x 6" L (10cm x 15cm).

Techniques to Try

- Depict something tiny in exaggerated internal proportions.
- Juxtapose an object in two different scales within one work of art.
- Choose two colors, one dull and neutral, one bright and lively. Create a balanced abstract composition and notice how much of each color you use.
- Create a work that is deliberately unbalanced.
- If you usually create work on a large scale, try something tiny or vice versa.
- Use exaggerated or contrasting internal proportions to emphasize one element in your artwork.

✳✳✳

When you are designing a quilt and it just doesn't seem to be coming together the way you'd like it to, remember to refer to your checklist to see if you've abided by these design principles. Are the colors playing well together or are they fighting? Is the balance off? What are the lines in your quilt conveying? Chances are, once you ask yourself these questions, you'll resolve the issue and the making of your quilt will be a joyful process!

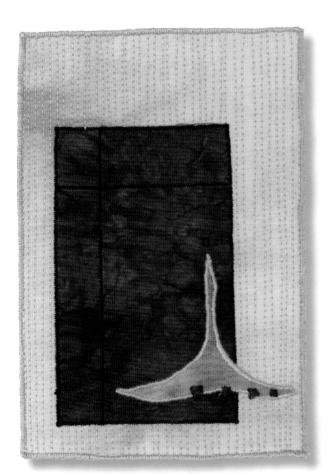

"Balance," 4" W x 6" L (10cm x 15cm). Asymmetrical balance is more casual and often much more complex. All of the elements of art and design must come into play, although many artists are able to create balance within their compositions by instinct. Look at Asian art and you will see a deliberate use of asymmetrical balance. A mountain will offset a tiny bird, but the line of a branch and the color of the bird will draw your eye around the artwork, creating a beautifully balanced composition.

Chapter Three
WAYS TO ASSEMBLE A QUILT

There are a number of exciting ways to assemble a unique quilt that do not require traditional piecing or appliqué skills. They're very helpful to know, but you don't have to master them before embarking on your art quilt journey. Assembling an art quilt top can be a lot of fun, whether you choose to fuse fabrics together, create with fabric collage, paint a quilt top, or use reverse appliqué. In this chapter some of the top artists in the art quilt world share their tips and tricks for easy and enjoyable quilt assembly.

"Betty's Bloomers #5," 13" W x 16" L (33cm x 41cm).

Fused Quilts

Laura Wasilowski

FUSING IS THE TRANSFER OF FUSIBLE WEBBING (a dry glue) to fabric by means of an iron. Once the webbing is transferred to the fabric, it can be cut into any shape you like and "re-fused" to another fabric. It is a fast, easy way to create fabric artwork and still maintain your sanity. A fused fabric cut on the bias may be manipulated into curves, waves, loops, and woven patterns. These organic shapes and textures lend activity and lively pattern to the quilt surface. The best part about a bias fused fabric? It doesn't fray. Following are instructions for practicing fusing on the bias with my quilt design "Betty's Bloomers," inspired by my sister's flower gardens in Colorado. Enjoy the exploration of bias fusing and expand your fusing repertoire!

Tips for Fusing

- Follow the manufacturer's recommendations for heat settings and time recommendations for fusing. The instructions come with the fusible webbing—read them. Some fabrics with a permanent press or other finish will not adhere to fusible web. Choose 100% cotton fabrics with no finish; hand-dyed fabrics work best.

- Wash and iron your fabric to remove any sizing before fusing. Do not use fabric softener.
  Note: Permanent press finishes do not wash out.

- Don't worry about the fabric bubbling when you fuse; it will flatten out when the paper is peeled off and the fabric is fused to another fabric.

- Don't worry about the webbing separating from the release paper before it is used. Just place the webbing on the fabric and the release paper on top and fuse into place.

- Fuse large sheets of fabric and store them by rolling the fabric up with the release paper still on the fabric.

- Always let the fabric and webbing cool and rest for at least fifteen minutes before trying to remove the paper.

- Peel the paper off the fused fabric before cutting. This will save your scissors and cutting blades from dulling and save hours of tedious paper peeling.

- Always use sharp scissors. Dull scissors fray the fabric.

- If you need to leave the paper on when cutting out a pattern piece, remove it by gently slicing the paper in the center of the fabric with the tip of your scissors and popping the paper off.

- Try to remove the release paper in one piece by first fanning a finger, then your hand, between the fabric and paper as if you were lifting cookies from a cookie sheet.

- Save the large sheets of release paper from the fusible webbing. This paper can be fused to over and over again. It is perfect for assembling fused collage and patternmaking.

- When cutting a stack of fused fabric, do not place fused sides together or they may be difficult to separate.

- When fusing two different fabrics together, and whenever possible, place dark-colored fabrics on top of light-value fabrics; dark fabrics may cast a shadow if placed under light-value fabrics. Fuse elements lightly, with little pressure, until you are satisfied with the arrangement. This way the elements can be easily removed or, when using release paper, will not lose their fusibility.

- Save all of your fused scraps. They are great for tiny elements and collage work.

- And most important, always keep your shiny side down. Do not allow the fusible webbing or the fused side of the fabric to touch a hot iron.

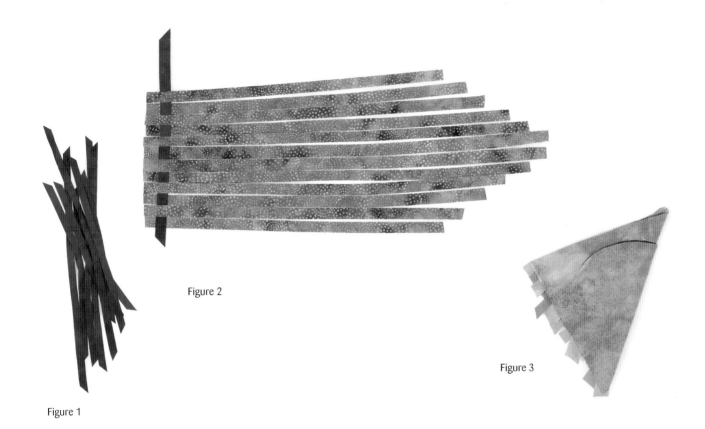

Figure 2

Figure 3

Figure 1

Techniques to Try

Materials

- 1 yard (1 meter) of fusible webbing (I prefer Wonder-Under.)
- 14" x 14" (36cm x 36cm) green fabric for tablecloth
- 12" x 12" (31cm x 31cm) blue fabric for tablecloth
- 4" x 4" (10cm x 10cm) orange fabric for vase
- 5" x 5" (13cm x 13cm) light blue fabric for vase stripes
- 16" x 18" (41cm x 46cm) very light green fabric for background
- 6" x 6" (15cm x 15cm) dark green fabric for leaves
- 6" x 6" (15cm x 15cm) medium green fabric for curlicues
- 6" x 6" (15cm x 15cm) red fabric for flower petals
- 2" x 6" (5cm x 15cm) green fabric for flower centers
- 2" x 6" (5cm x 15cm) yellow fabric for flower centers
- 16" x 18" (41cm x 46cm) batting
- 16" x 18" (41cm x 46cm) backing
- Machine-quilting thread
- Rotary cutter with regular and pinking blades
- Teflon pressing sheet
- Small wand iron

OPTIONAL

- 14" x 16" (36cm x 41cm) fusible stiff interfacing (I prefer fast2fuse.)
- Size 8 embroidery thread

PREPARATION

Fuse all the fabrics and remove all the release paper except for the paper on the background fabric. Save the paper for construction of quilt elements. Or in place of release paper, use a Teflon pressing sheet.

Note: A bias-cut strip is cut at a 45-degree angle from the grain of the fabric or from corner to corner on a square piece of fabric.

DIRECTIONS

Tablecloth and Vase

STEP 1: Cut 12 bias strips measuring about ½" (1cm) wide by 14" (36cm) or longer from the green tablecloth fabric. Trim the ends square.

STEP 2: Cut 16 bias strips measuring about ½" (1cm) wide by 10" (26cm) or longer from the blue tablecloth fabric **(Figure 1)**.

STEP 3: Align the 12 green strips horizontally on the release paper and fuse-tack ½" (1cm) of the right side of each strip onto the paper.

STEP 4: Weave the 16 blue strips vertically through the horizontal strips, fuse-tacking each vertical strip as it is woven. Try curving the horizontal strips as you weave to make an undulating pattern. After the fabric cools remove it from the paper **(Figure 2)**.

STEP 5: Trim the tablecloth collage to measure about 6"x 9" (15cm x 23cm). Curve the edges as you trim.

STEP 6: Cut 10 bias strips measuring about ⅛" (.3cm) wide and tapering to ½" (1cm) from the light blue vase stripes fabric.

Figure 4

Figure 5

Figure 6

STEP 7: Fuse-tack the orange vase square onto release paper. Place the end of a bias vase strip ¼" (.6cm) beyond one corner of the square and fuse-tack the end into place. Slowly curve and fuse the strip across the square to the opposite corner. Repeat with the remaining bias strips, spacing them across the square. After the fabric cools, remove it from the paper. Trim off the extending strips.

STEP 8: Fold the vase square from corner to corner to form a triangle. Cut a large curved arc to form a circle when opened. Cut a small scoop from the top of the circle for the vase opening **(Figure 3)**.

STEP 9: Center the tablecloth at an angle on the lower part of the background fabric and place the vase on top. Fuse-tack into place, but leave 1" (3cm) free at the vase opening so the leaves can be slipped under the rim **(Figure 4)**.

Flowers, Leaves, and Curlicues

STEP 1: Cut 5 bias strips tapering from a sharp point to ½" (1cm) wide from the dark green leaf fabric **(Figure 5)**.

STEP 2: Cut 7 bias strips measuring about ⅛" (.3cm) wide from the light green curlicue fabric **(Figure 6)**.

STEP 3: Slip the wide end of the 5 dark green leaves just under the rim of the vase. Fuse-tack just at the base of the leaves.

STEP 4: Fuse each leaf individually by curving the leaf with one hand while fusing with the other. *Note:* A small wand iron is handy for this task.

STEP 5: Add the light green strips to the leaves and fuse individually by curving and gently curling the strip as you fuse.

STEP 6: Cut 5 strips measuring about 1" (3cm) wide by 6" (15cm) long from the flower petal fabric with the pinking rotary cutter blade **(Figure 7)**.

STEP 7: Snip a total of 55 triangles measuring about ½" (1cm) wide on the decorative side from the strips in Step 6.

STEP 8: Cut 11 dots measuring about ¾" (2cm) wide from the green flower center fabric and 11 dots measuring about ½" (1cm) from the yellow flower center fabric.

STEP 9: Arrange 5 flower petals in a circle on the release paper. Place a green dot on top to engage the petals. Add a yellow dot in the center and fuse-tack into place. Repeat with the remaining flower parts to make a total of 11 flowers. After the fabric cools, remove from the paper.

STEP 10: Arrange the flowers on the quilt top. Fuse-tack into place.

STEP 11: Remove the release paper from the background fabric. Steam set the quilt top to the batting and quilt backing.

✳✳✳

Finishing the Quilt

There are several ways to finish your quilt. The first option is to machine or hand-quilt. Trim the quilt square, add a rod pocket and binding. The second option is to add decorative handstitching just through the batting layer. Wrap the quilt top around the fast2fuse interfacing to the back and fuse. Machine quilt, then add a fused backing and hanging loop for display.

Fusible webbing opens up a world of quick, fun, and appealing design opportunities. Take time to experiment with the variety of fusible products available. You'll learn which ones work best for the fabrics you are using. Then have fun creating!

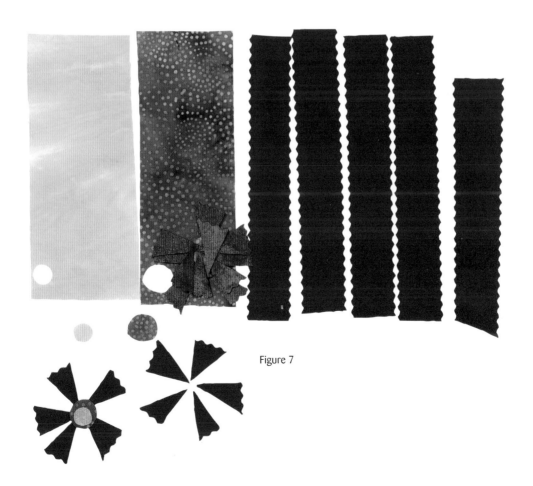

Figure 7

"Moonrise," 11.5" W x 12.5" L (29cm x 32cm).

Reverse Appliqué

Deana Hartman

I FIND REVERSE APPLIQUÉ especially liberating. When the design process has finished, I find that cutting away the layers of the fabric not used makes it much easier to bead and embellish.

This quick method for reverse appliqué by machine can certainly be addictive and lends itself to hand embellishing, since cutting away the fabrics means fewer layers of fabric to pull the needle through. Experiment with a variety of fabrics, prints, and color schemes to see what you can reveal with this process.

Technique to Try

Materials
- ◘ Two contrasting fabrics
- ◘ Writing instrument
- ◘ Straight pins
- ◘ Sewing machine
- ◘ Threads
- ◘ Fabric scissors
- ◘ Decorative yarns (optional)

DIRECTIONS

STEP 1: Choose the fabric that will be on top. On the fabric, create a design using the writing instrument you prefer. You might try a grid, curves, spirals, or other simple shapes.

STEP 2: Layer the fabrics and baste with straight pins. Be sure to leave the fabric on which you've drawn your design on the top.

STEP 3: Straight stitch your design with a walking foot, free-motion foot, or regular machine quarter-inch foot, depending on the complexity and shapes of your design.

STEP 4: Remove the straight pins. From the front of the fabric, begin cutting out layers to reveal the other fabrics below. When cutting out the layers, cut up to about 1/16" (.2cm) to the straight stitching line.

STEP 5: When you are satisfied with the design effect, select a yarn for couching. Cover the straight stitching by couching down the yarn. It is the artist's choice whether the yarn completely covers the raw edge or not.

STEP 6: Once couching is complete, cut out any extra layers of fabric from the back of the piece so that only one layer of fabric remains. Save all of the cut-out shapes for other appliqué projects.

~tip~
❧ To couch yarn, use a couching foot to zigzag stitch over the yarn, covering the straight stitching. I use one hand to guide the yarn while the other hand guides the fabrics.

This textile piece consists of reverse appliqué. I love to layer patterned fabrics, then fray the edges I've cut away to create a vintage look.

Other Examples of Reverse Appliqué

Charlotte Liddle

FOR MY COLLECTION OF WORK titled "Souvenir from France" I used reverse appliqué to create fabric samples that reflect a country feel found from my research trip to Provence. In order to get a worn and torn effect, I layered up patterned fabrics, cut back through areas, and with a teasel brush gently frayed the edges for a distressed look. I enjoyed the looseness, freedom, and quality of line that this style of frayed appliqué and embroidery could produce.

I love to use pattern on pattern, unusual combinations of color, and interesting textured fabrics in my work. Reverse appliqué can produce interesting effects if done with two different patterned fabrics, especially if the scale and intensity of color within the patterns vary. For quite an abstract design layer, use up to three or more different fabrics and randomly select which areas you cut through—I've found this to be a great way of creating a surface to embellish.

Another great material to use with reverse appliqué is leather. At first glance this may sound a bit tricky, but the leather works well because it doesn't fray, it's pretty sturdy, and it's thick enough to add an extra dimension to flat design. I've made a fantastic leather bag this way. I love the way you can create such a clean outline by cutting through the leather to reveal a very busy bold vintage pattern underneath.

The possibilities are endless, and the best advice I can give is simply to give it a go. If you think it probably won't work, try it anyway. There's no harm in experimenting. I've created some of my best work through just playing, cutting up, and reworking. Always remember that some of the greatest designs weren't right the first time!

"Primordial Sea," 7½' W x 5' L (2m x 1m).

Wholecloth Design

Judy Coates Perez

Another option is to paint a design on the fabric surface to create a unique art quilt—no piecing, collage, or appliqué necessary. Think of painting an entire design on one piece of fabric, like it's a canvas. Imagery can be drawn and painted onto one piece of fabric, then enhanced with free-motion quilting, handstitching, and/or embellishment. In order to give wholecloth quilts texture and depth, quilting and thread choice play very important roles.

~tip~
✿ If you quilt too heavily in one area and not enough in other areas, you are more likely to end up with a quilt that does not lie or hang flat.

Fabric Collage
Katy Korkos

THOSE OF US WHO WANT to make things all have
something to say, things we've been thinking about.
My themes are about language, pattern recognition,
maps, and the inspiration I get from nature and
natural forms. Your thought patterns are probably
much different from mine, but whatever the theme,
it is always the thought behind the piece that
engages others.

I often use birds as a design motif in my work because of all the
things they symbolize to me: expressiveness, song, flight, beauty,
freedom, cages, nesting, the potential in an egg, living in the trees,
fragility, and strength. I have bird feeders outside my studio window, and I wake to the sound of ravens. I consider it a good omen
for my day if the red-tailed hawk is sitting on her telephone pole
when I drive to work; I enjoy the turkey vultures' wing-wobble and
the swallows' swoop.

You might have as your theme family, faith, romantic love, travel,
transportation, ecology, landscape, water, trees, wildlife, home—
you see what I'm getting at here. Even the most abstract or geometric quilt has come from the thoughts of the artist. Someone
using circles might be thinking about life cycles, cells, the encircl-
ing protection of a family, targets, coming full circle, circular logic,
or the full moon, but if she is not thinking about what she's doing,
it will just be a quilt and won't be art. It won't convey anything but
"quilt" to the viewer.

My goal is to make a clear statement, but not in the sense that a
political poster might make a statement. The work I like best has
intrigue, shows evidence that it was made by hand, and demon-
strates the passage of time.

See the following project for ideas on creating a collage on fabric.

"Raven Dictionary," 20¼" W x 56½" L (51cm x 144cm).

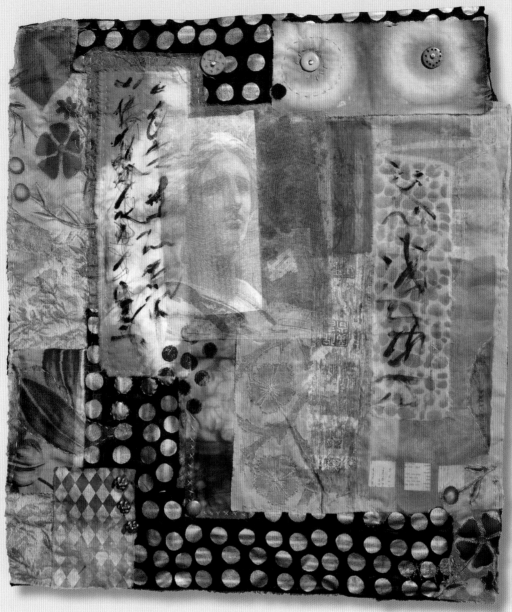

"Silence,"
23¾" W x 26¼" L
(60cm x 67cm).

Techniques to Try

DIRECTIONS

STEP 1: Think of what you want to say, your theme, your thoughts, your soul, and keep it uppermost in your mind as you work on the piece. Your voice will come through, even in the most abstract pieces.

STEP 2: Choose a color scheme and stick to it; try not to be distracted by all of the beautiful colors at your disposal. Color can help create harmony in a collage that by definition will include a lot of other varying elements.

STEP 3: Gather your materials: fabrics, images, papers, trims, yarns, paints, stamps, embellishments, sewing machine, and anything else you want to include.

NOTE: The type of paint (or marking product) you use doesn't matter for wall hangings; it could be acrylic, fabric paint, pastel or charcoal on dampened fabric, oil stick, diluted bleach on dark fabric, crayon, mud, or rusty wire.

STEP 4: Choose a background fabric with some texture or printing that will immediately bring interest to the piece. Batiks are good commercial fabrics for this purpose.

STEP 5: Add complex elements that differ in texture, type of mark, and scale, all while keeping your theme in mind. Now you can really begin to compose.

"Bouquet of Tulips," 18½" W x 30" L (47cm x 76cm).

STEP 6: As you compose, state your theme, then vary the theme and repeat it. For example, say your theme is travel. You might start with a piece of commercial fabric that's preprinted with a map motif. Then you might scan and print related elements onto fabric, such as photos and text. And you might use the quilting to emphasize certain design elements, such as lines of the roadways.

STEP 7: Try not to prejudge as you add elements. Be free in your first few moves and sew, fuse, or pin the pieces down to get the dialog going. You can always make changes if the elements don't work.

STEP 8: Let your art speak to you; let it tell you what it needs next. Let it take its own time. Few of us live in a world where we can create whenever the muse strikes, but avoid trying to force a color or embellishment to work because you have to leave for a doctor's appointment in ten minutes. The collage will be there when you get back, and the perfect solution may have occurred to you by then, too.

STEP 9: Crop as you compose. Remember, nothing is precious, and everything can be reused. The composition needs to please you, the artist. Did I put that bird right smack dab in the middle? Did I mean to do that, and is that the kind of composition I like? If it isn't, I chop something off the side or bottom, or add an equally strong bird off center, to balance it out.

STEP 10: Integrate the layers. For me this means beginning to stitch, by hand or machine, to make the piece look like it belongs together, that my design elements are not just stuck on top. I might layer transparent fabrics such as organza or lace over the top of elements where the transition is too abrupt between foreground and background, using the fabric like a painter uses a glaze.

STEP 11: Know when to take a step back, literally and figuratively. When the process starts feeling less intuitive, less joyful, I like to stop and take a walk, breathe deeply, gaze at some water or a tree, pet the dog, put on some loud music and boogie around the studio, or drink some coffee. Then I look at the work again, sometimes with reversed binoculars or I take a picture and look at the image, not the piece itself. Sometimes I put it away for a few days and wait to see if anything occurs to me while I'm not looking at the collage.

STEP 12: The quilting process, or merely tying the layers together, can be an opportunity for improving your piece. Quilting can be texture, line, a new top layer, a way of integrating the surface even more, or a way to tone down the piece (by using a contrasting color) or brighten up the piece (by using a heightened color of thread).

STEP 13: Although you don't want to rush your art, you might want to set a reasonable deadline for completing it. Finishing the work is the hardest part for me, mostly because I have enjoyed the process so much and I don't ever want it to end. I attend a critique group monthly and a regional group of the Studio Art Quilt Associates (SAQA) bimonthly, and that helps me to finish my pieces and get them ready for presentation. Having deadlines for competitions and exhibits also helps me bring the work to a close.

~tip~

✐ Limiting the palette makes the work seem more serious. I don't mean you can't use twenty different hues of olive green or grayish lavender or that strange pinkish brown, but if you choose a color scheme that has red, orange, yellow, green, blue, and violet in it, it should have some relevance to your work.

Even though it's your creation, and yours to make perfect if you wish, it's also an expression of the creativity that is flowing through you, and the process is as important as, if not more important than, the final product. Try not to be too judgmental. If you really need another opinion, show the piece to someone you trust (in an artistic sense) and ask him or her what he or she thinks it means—keeping in mind that art is open to interpretation.

Finally, ask yourself: "Did I say what I was trying to say?" If so, then that's what matters.

"A Bird," 17" W x 20¾" L (43cm x 53cm), unmounted.

"Groovy Guitars," 35" W x 55" L (89cm x 140cm).

Free-Motion Quilting

Robbi Joy Eklow

FOR SOME PEOPLE, quilting is a means to hold the quilt together. For me, the opposite is true: The quilt is there to keep the quilting thread from flying off into space. My quilts are made from hand-dyed fabrics that I have put together using fused raw edge appliqué, and because my quilt tops are generally pretty simple, I rely on intricate free-motion machine quilting to draw the viewer in closer.

My free-motion quilting designs consist of motifs that are generally about 1" (3cm) square, with a different motif being used in each shape. More complex motifs, such as flowers, are slightly larger, maybe 2" (5cm) square. I coordinate the color of the thread to the color of the shape on the quilt, and change both color and motif when moving from shape to shape. I avoid using the same motifs on adjoining shapes. If one shape has a motif with curves, the shape next to it has one with straight lines.

To practice these methods, see Techniques on the next page. Gather the following supplies:

* Sixteen 9" x 12" (23cm x 31cm) rectangles of felt (any color)
Before I start quilting one of my fused quilts, I warm up on either a sample square or on two pieces of felt stacked together. Felt makes an excellent practice surface, since it's cheap, allowing you to throw it away without feeling bad. Felt pieces are also perfect for testing new motifs.

* Sewing machine
All your machine has to do is move the needle up and down and give you good tension. Set it up for free-motion stitching. I drop the feed dogs; if you can't or don't want to, just set your stitch length to zero. You will be controlling the stitches, not the machine. It's as if the machine is the pencil, and you are moving the paper. If you have a straight-stitch plate, now's the time to use it. It helps avoid skipped stitches.

* Foot
You will need either a free-motion embroidery foot or a darning foot. I prefer a foot with an open circle. The open toe lets you see what you are doing and you can back up if you have managed to sew your foot into your quilt. Make sure your foot clears the surface of the quilt when the needle is up; some feet still put pressure on the quilt, but you want to be able to move the quilt freely when the needle is not sticking into the quilt.

* Thread
I prefer polyester or rayon machine-embroidery thread, 40-weight. Wind a bobbin full of the same thread you will use in the needle. I like to use a thread stand to allow the thread to feed off the top of the spool. I have been having good success with Isacord polyester embroidery thread; it comes in myriad colors and the spool stands up on its own.

* Needle
I use both Schmetz embroidery needles, size 75, or Organ titanium sharps, size 12. Both of these needles help keep the thread from shredding.

* Eye protection
I wear my bifocals while quilting. I'd rather not have a needle come flying into my eye.

Techniques to Try

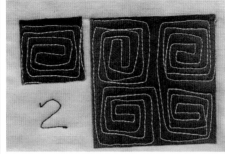

Sample 1

This is the easiest and most versatile of all the motifs. Start at the upper left corner, move down, move over to the right, go back up, move over to the right. When you've done about a 1" (3cm) square, change the proportions, so the longer lengths are going vertically. If you aren't in a good place to start another square, stitch a straight line along the outside of the squares you've made until you get to where you want to be.

Sample 2

A square turned into a spiral. Start at the upper left, move right to the edge of the square, and move down just short of the edge of the square, leaving enough room for the line of stitching on the return trip. Then turn left, leave enough room again for the return trip, and go back. Each time, leave room for the return trip. When you get to the center, turn around and come out between the "lane" you left before.

Sample 3

This sample is the same as Sample 2 except that you move in a circle to create curved spirals. The trip into the center is clockwise; come out counterclockwise. You can fill almost any shape with a spiral—just follow along the edges, leaving room for a return trip. You can also make the return trip squiggly.

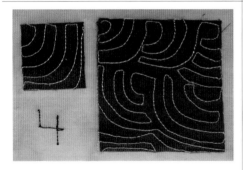

Sample 4

Similar to Sample 1, you are just curving the long lines to create a "fan." Start at the center with a short arc, and make the lines longer each time. When they get too long, they get messy, so do only about six arcs, and then start a new fan, using the edges of the quilt shape and the last line you quilted as boundaries for the arcs.

Sample 5

I call this "garlic." Start at the upper left corner, make a small clockwise loop, then switch directions and make a counterclockwise loop around it. Then repeat. Start a new "garlic" whenever you want. I don't have the loops all go back to the beginning of that specific motif; they "bounce" off of previously made loops.

Sample 6

This is the same as Sample 5, except that the tops of the loops are pointy.

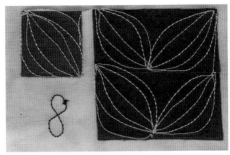

Sample 7

This leafy design reminds me of waltzing. You take one step forward, one step back, then one step forward, through the center of the shape you just made.

Sample 8

This is similar to Sample 7. Just take the back and forth steps a few more times before moving on.

Sample 9

Same as Sample 7, except this time, make a spiral during the last forward step. You can vary this motif infinitely by doing all kinds of interesting things within that shape created by the first two steps.

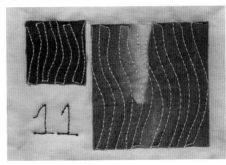

Sample 10

This is similar to Sample 9, except the spiral comes in the second step. You can make this follow a line. Echo the outline to get back to the beginning of the line if you want to do another row.

Sample 11

Curved lines are easier to repeat gracefully than straight lines.

Sample 12

Make the ends of the lines pointy, then start curving them enough to "bounce off" the last line. Work in sections going up and down.

Sample 13
Combine a spiral with straight lines to make flowers or suns.

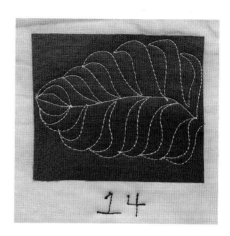

Sample 14
The spiky lines in Sample 12 can become a feather. With a chalk marker, draw a curvy horizontal guideline from left to right. Start this feather at the center left edge, making spiky curves running along the line. Make them bigger as you move toward the right. This creates the top of the feather. When you are at the right edge, stitch directly along the drawn line, then form the bottom of the feather by making spiky curves along the bottom half. After a while, you won't need the guideline. You can also use the edge of a shape as a guideline and move up and down it, building up the design to fill space.

Sample 15
Make more flowers, form a center spiral, and make the spiky lines go back and forth around the spiral.

Sample 16
Combine curved long lines and leafy shapes to make a design that looks like wood.

Practice and see what new motifs you can come up with.

Tips for Stitching

- Start quilting in the center and work your way to the edges, then trim the quilt to size when you are done. As I use small motifs and only concentrate on a small portion of the quilt at a time, I don't have to move the entire quilt from top to bottom or side to side while I work. I am only concerned with the 3" (8cm) or 4" (10cm) area I am about to quilt. I bunch the quilt up and shove it into the machine, leaving just the working area free.

- Grip the quilt with your fists. I don't use my hands flat on the work surface as some people do. Because I can get a good grip on the quilt, I don't need special gloves or a free-motion quilting guide. The quilt does not have to be flat on the surface of the machine—the only part that has to be flat is what is directly under the needle, and the foot takes care of that.

- Devise a way to support the weight of your quilt (like a long, flat table) so that the weight of the quilt is not pulling against the needle.

- Don't worry about a consistent stitch length; this comes with practice. Concern yourself more with striving for a smooth, rhythmic line. Also, don't worry about crossing stitch paths. I cross them all of the time.

- For thread, I choose to have the needle thread and the bobbin thread match. Even when the tension is adjusted perfectly, you will see both threads. I don't ever use clear thread; I like the thread to be visible.

- When you are in the middle of the quilt, it's easier to move the quilt up and down than from side to side. I usually start with a vertically oriented pattern. On patterns with corners, I find myself using one hand to control the "up-down" movement, the other to move the quilt from side to side.

- I space my free-motion lines about ¼" (.6cm) apart. You might want to work a little larger. It takes me about an hour to fill up one square foot of quilting. You can use the edge of your presser foot as a guide and glide it along the edge of the shape or along the last line quilted. That is one reason I prefer a smaller foot to a larger foot.

- Don't look at the needle when you are quilting; look at the line you are drawing on the quilt. No one except you knows what you meant to do. This is not billiards, in which you have to say what you plan to do before you try to do it. If you are striving for a motif and it morphs into another shape, go with it. If you get bored filling space with one motif, then switch to another. The final effect is all that matters. Sometimes I try to make a feather and end up with a flower. That's fine with me.

Chapter Four
EMBELLISHED AND MIXED-MEDIA QUILTING

Today the options for embellishment are limitless; artists are using a variety of media and techniques to create unique, whimsical, and stunning works of art—anything goes these days, as long as it can be stitched. And with so many artists "going green" by recycling quilt scraps and objects that would otherwise be thrown away, artists have found a way to express their environmental concerns with fabric and stitch. In this chapter, fiber artists demystify media and explore exciting ways to make your quilts stand out.

Embellishing with Attitude:
FOUND OBJECTS

Pamela Allen

I ADMIT IT: I'LL USE ANYTHING to embellish a quilt. In fact, if it can be drilled, punched, or glued to a button, it's an embellishment in my book. Embellished quilts have every kind of embellishment nowadays––from beads and buttons to found objects and dollhouse furniture. If the embellishment can be adhered in some fashion to your quilt, go ahead and explore using it!

Coming to fabric art from a fine-art background is a mixed blessing. I am still working and practicing so that I might perfect techniques that are second nature to quilters. On the other hand, I feel I have an advantage in that I have a particular method for developing an image that has served me well for many years. And my ignorance of the "rules" has encouraged an attitude that anything goes as long as it contributes to the intent of the work.

I have a vast collection of oddities from my former life as a mixed-media artist. These may not immediately say "embellishment" to most people, but to me they are irresistible for enriching the narrative of my work. Plastic frogs, bugs, and toys—even if tacky and ugly—can be transformed with gold leaf. Wooden, metal, and plastic can all be pierced with the proper tools. Sculpey clay can be molded into any shape. Impossibly hard or odd-shaped items can be glued to shank buttons and then sewn on.

"Grandmother's Lullaby," 33" W x 45" L (84cm x 114cm).

When thinking of embellishments for your quilts, think of the subject. What things symbolize this person or this way of life? Why not attach keys, food, clothespins, curlers, kitchen utensils, jewelry, writing implements, and anything else that represents your person or theme? If it's about eating, then go ahead and sew on some fruit, vegetables, knives, and forks . . . even a cork from a wine bottle. Why not? You will never shop at dollar stores, flea markets, and thrift shops in the same way once you begin an embellishment collection to rival your fabric stash.

I start each of my projects with only a vague idea of where I'm going. I use whatever I have on hand, drawing on my small stash of mainly recycled and thrift shop fabrics.

In this example, a sarong offers the suggestion of a window, door, or piece of furniture. The foreground becomes the tabletop, with an oversized plate to provide lots of room for future additions. The fabric is appliquéd with embroidery floss.

DIRECTIONS

STEP 1: Start with the whole quilt sandwich: back, batting, and top. This gives you something substantial to work with and allows the handsewing to become part of the texture of the work. I make a background by overlapping shapes, textures, and colors until I am pleased with the composition.

STEP 2: Once you're happy with the placement, commit to it and baste it using spray adhesive (making sure to mask off any area you do not want to get glue on), or even use a glue stick to adhere the pieces.

STEP 3: Raw-edge appliqué the quilt by hand, using embroidery floss and the ladder stitch. This creates some texture, and the colored line enhances the image. Usually this background begins to tell me what the next step will be. If the shapes are horizontal and vertical, then maybe the design is an interior. Flowing and organic? It could be a landscape. Once an idea starts to emerge, I can begin to construct an image with more fabric shapes. In this example, horizontals and verticals suggested the subject of a table set for a meal. I added a fish on a plate and had my theme: "Fish and Chips."

Technique to Try

Materials

- Any fabric combination you fancy—recycled old thrift shop clothes; mixtures and specialty fabrics; cottons, rayons, and polyesters; prints or solids
- Batting—poly or cotton
- Spray baste or glue stick
- Sewing machine for free-motion quilting
- Handsewing implements such as needles, thread, and so on
- Embellishments of all kinds (Some of my favorites include plastic frogs and bugs, safety pins, artificial fruits and flowers, corks, old jewelry, keys, garters, plastic bird's eggs, bones, miniature anything, toys, wooden wheels.)
- Beads, buttons, and sequins

OPTIONAL

- Dremel tool for drilling holes
- Two-hole metal punch
- Gold size and gold leaf
- Five-minute epoxy glue
- White glue
- Water-base crystal-finish varnish

In this example, a few more fabric elements enhance the image, and then the entire surface is machine quilted.

Unusual embellishments can engage the viewer. If the baubles and quilting are related to the image, it adds to the pleasure of looking.

STEP 4: Now it is time to machine quilt the surface. I like to treat the quilting as a further element in the composition rather than just something used to add pattern. In the "Fish and Chips" piece, I quilted in some plant forms as well as a grid to reinforce the idea of a tablecloth. Adding a bubbly motif in the background gives some interesting contrast to the simple planes of the tabletop. *Note:* Bind your quilt and put a sleeve and label on the back before you embellish. Those lumpy vegetables and kitchen utensils get in the way, otherwise.

STEP 5: Now for the fun! The secret to unique embellishment is to consider anything that might be interesting or contribute to the image. There will always be a way to attach such things. I choose embellishments in two categories: one is purely decorative, such as the beads in the corners of the diamond grid; the other is used to enhance the theme of the narrative. Here I have used artificial carrots, peas, and a lemon for the dinner menu. These I often find at dollar stores, and I buy the ones made of Styrofoam with a plastic skin. They are easy to cut in half with an X-acto knife and thus lay flat on the surface. The "skin" is tough enough to sew through without shredding. The carrots are affixed with a single bead to avoid exposing the thread. The spine of the fish is made with real

fish vertebrae (why not?) alternating with beads. I couldn't resist thinking of the chips as poker chips, so I drilled holes with a Dremel tool, applied gold leaf, and arranged them on the plate. Having pierced the knife and fork, they too were sewn on. I wanted to pay attention to the outside of the rectangle as well, so I devised a fringe of fishing lures and poker chips for the bottom edge. Some velvet leaves finished off the flowers.

Embellishment Ideas

* **Sculpey polymer clay is remarkable stuff.** You can use it to make molds of simple shapes such as doll hands or a mouth from a mask. These can be used to make any number of the same item on demand. After being baked (in a toaster oven for twenty minutes), hardened polymer clay can be drilled, painted, or gilded, and it's ready to sew on a quilt.
* **Buttons with shanks become little platforms upon which anything can be glued and then stitched to a quilt.** Items such as dice, watch parts, or pebbles too hard or awkward to drill can be attached to the flat side of a button with five-minute epoxy glue. Buttons are also useful when découpaged with an image and then finished with high-gloss water-based varnish.
* **Bones make wonderful organic and symbolic embellishments.** A chicken dinner can yield a variety of bones. Once boiled and allowed to dry, they can be varnished and then drilled for easy attachment.
* **Beads by the yard, or even Mardi Gras beads, are convenient for outlining a form quickly.** They can be couched on using contrasting embroidery floss between the beads to add another touch of color.
* **Beaded fringe by the yard is also a fun and easy addition.** It makes dangling, swishing hair when sewn in rows and can be doubled to create a thicker fringe.
* **Your quilt can even jingle! I use jingle bells of many sizes and colors to add the element of sound.** Remember to use strong beading thread to prevent the metal from cutting through.

Before you go out and buy more beads or other embellishments, have a look around your house to see what you have on hand and can place into your embellished quilt. Perhaps you'll rethink throwing away your children's collection of miniature race cars, that pair of old prescription glasses, or your mother's collection of vintage spoons. Remember, anything goes!

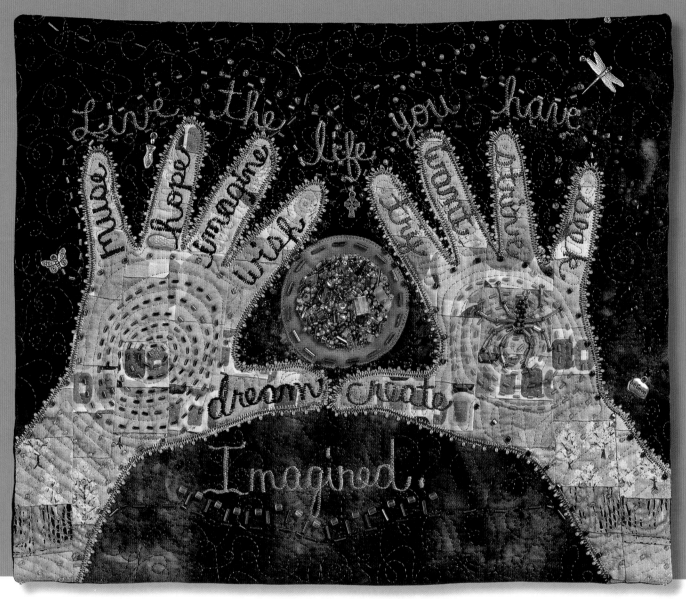

"She's Got the Moon," 14" W x 11.5" L (36cm x 30cm).

The Need to Bead: Bead Collage
Deana Hartman

BEADS HAVE BEEN AROUND for thousands of years. Whether made of glass, clay, paper, metal, shell, animal teeth, or stone, beads still cast their secret magic over us today. Recognized for their beauty and value in years past, some cultures used them as currency. Other societies used beads as status symbols, to ward off evil spirits, to make political statements, or to bring good luck. Bead collage is a modern way to add meaning and texture to fiber artwork. This three-dimensional art form can be used on art quilts, clothing, jewelry pieces, and other fiber applications.

Making a Bead Stew

A successful bead stew will consist of beads, sequins, and charms. Not unlike its food-based counterpart, bead variety is essential for a successful stew. Think colors and shades, finishes (such as matte, silver-lined, rainbow, opaque), and size. Here are some recipe suggestions:

❋ THE BROTH
Size 10, 8, and 6 glass seed beads

❋ THE SEASONINGS
Glass bugle beads, pewter charms

❋ THE VEGETABLES
Cube, triangle, and hexagon beads in various colors, sizes, and finishes; sequins in various shapes, sizes, and colors; medium and large glass beads

❋ THE MEAT
Unique or focal beads (usually purchased individually). Ideas for focal beads include lamp, furnace-glass, cloisonné, ceramic, or even fabric beads.

Preparing to Bead

First, create or purchase a bead collage mix (bead stew) that complements the background to be covered. It is important that the bead stew has color elements similar to those of the background. The color match will make it unnecessary to cover every inch of space with beads, and it will camouflage the less-beaded areas. To prepare your surface for bead collage, it is best to begin with three layers of fibers such as a quilted surface or a fiber sandwich (front and back fabrics with cotton batting in between). Because layers of beading can become heavy, the additional fibers help stabilize the bead collage and keep the tension even.

To start, choose the area for the bead collage. This may be a free-form shape or a particular form such as a flower center, moon, or other part of the design to be filled in. Before you decide which beads to use where, remember that bead collage is a series of steps in which you work from large to small scale.

You will want to apply larger beads, charms, and sequin sets first, using the running and stop stitches. Work in a small area, about 2" (5cm) in any direction before moving to the next area. Begin by adding in seed and bugle combinations, large beads, stop-stitched bead/sequin combinations, and charms. These should be no farther than ¼" (.6cm) to ⅛" (.3cm) apart.

Use a 24" (61cm) to 36" (92cm) length of Silamide beading thread. Double the length and knot the end. Bring the threaded needle from the back of the work to the front to begin beading. When your thread is running short, bring the needle to the back of the work. Knot closely to the back fabric, then take a stitch to help bury it. Snip the threads close to the last stitch taken.

Stitches

There are three stitches needed for bead collage: running, stop, and collage couching.

RUNNING STITCH

The running stitch is used for general bead application to apply single beads of most any size as well as a combination of small sets of beads to fabric. To make a line of running stitches, bring the needle up and repeat.

Single Bead Application

After bringing the threaded needle from the back of the work to the front, load the needle with a seed or bugle bead. Take a stitch just slightly smaller than the length of the bead. Stitch through all layers of the fiber piece. Bring the needle up in the next area for a new bead.

"Meaning of Life, Part 1," 7¾" x 7¾" (20cm x 20cm).

STOP STITCH

The stop stitch allows for the application of beads with one hole, such as a sequin, but can also be used for applying buttons and bead combinations.

To apply a sequin, bring the threaded needle from the back to the front. Load a sequin and a seed bead onto the needle. Stitch back through the sequin hole, but not the seed bead. The seed bead will act like a "stop bead" to keep the thread from going back through both the sequin and the bead.

COLLAGE COUCHING

After larger beads and stop stitches are applied to the fiber surface, strings of smaller seed beads are mortared between the large beads using the collage-couching stitch. Collage couching is the most essential part of the overall look of the bead collage. It "cements" all of the other elements together, tricks the eye, and builds texture and dimension in the piece.

"Flower Power," 15" W x 12" L (39cm x 31cm).

To begin, bring the threaded needle from the back to the front. Select from 5 to 13 small seed beads, making a string of them. Vary the seed and small bugles so there is no distinguishable pattern in the string for the eye to follow. Never put the same beads next to each other in a string of beads for collage.

Take a stitch as long as the set of seed beads, laying the string between larger beads and sequin combinations. Take one to three couching stitches along the length of the string of beads to secure them in place. The stitch should come up on one side of the string and go back down on the other. The thread will naturally slip in between the beads and be hidden from view.

Don't be afraid to overlap collaged strings to help cover or fill in the empty areas and add height to the work. Some purchased bead mixes consist of only seed and bugle beads. You will need to supplement these with a variety of medium to large beads and sequins for this technique.

~tips~

For additional texture ideas, try these techniques:
✿ Fuse on fabric shapes for design.
✿ Hand-dye threads for additional stitching before or after the bead collage is created.
✿ Hand-dye cheesecloth for depth and interest. This would be applied to the background before the bead collage is started.

Mixed-media needle felted sampler, 12" x 12" (31cm x 31cm).

Quilting and Needlefelting
Beryl Taylor

MACHINE NEEDLEFELTING HAS RECENTLY BECOME A FAVORITE ACTIVITY of mine; it lends itself to experimentation and the results are unpredictable, making it a very exciting process. It's also very easy to do. Needlefelting is the simple act of blending and adhering fibers by punching them repeatedly with a barbed needle. People often think that felting only applies to wool or silk roving, but that isn't the case. With machine needlefelting, almost any soft fibers or fabric can be felted together.

From a distance, a needlefelting machine looks like a sewing machine; however, it doesn't sew. Instead of having a top thread and a bobbin thread, a needlefelting machine has a cluster of very sharp barbed needles whose sole task is to punch fabrics together when you press down on the foot control. The results can be so beautiful, it gives a sense of instant gratification.

One aspect that I greatly enjoy is the layering effect that can be achieved with needlefelting. It is possible to add as many layers of fabrics as you like (dependent on the needles physically being able to cope), building up depth and texture as you go. When many layers are used, the fabrics and colors blend into each other, depending on how long you work on the piece with the felting machine, creating an exciting fabric for stitch.

In this section are directions for creating a small 12" x 12" (31cm x 31cm) needlefelted and embellished quilt with a simple geometric scheme. Whether you follow my instructions closely or loosely, the following activity will expand your needlefelting skills.

Technique to Try

Materials

- 12" x 12" (31cm x 31cm) piece of felt. This piece could be craft felt, hand-dyed wool felt, etc.
- Fabrics for needlefelting: polyesters, organzas, cheesecloth, scrim, etc.
- Fabric scissors
- Angelina fibers
- Beads
- Gold thread
- Silk ribbon for binding
- China silk fabric for backing
- Sewing machine with free-motion abilities
- Hand threads and needles

DIRECTIONS

STEP 1: Begin needlefelting felt diamond shapes onto a felt background. Then needlefelt a felt square onto the diamond, followed by a felt circle on the very top.

STEP 2: Turn the piece over and needlefelt the entire piece. This will help to integrate all of the various fabrics, while also bringing more of the base color into the piece.

STEP 3: Place snippets of Angelina fibers onto the individual circles and needlefelt them into place.

STEP 4: Lay some hand-dyed silk gauze over the whole piece and needlefelt around the diamonds.

STEP 5: Handstitch around the small square shapes with a silk thread.

STEP 6: Cut separate diamond shapes from silk chiffon and needlefelt them onto the diamond shaped panels that have not already been felted.

STEP 7: Bead around the edges of the chiffon both for decorative purposes and to help to secure the chiffon into position.

STEP 8: Using gold thread, stitch around the diamond shapes and stitch a bead at each point of the diamond.

STEP 9: Back the panel with China silk in a coordinating color, and bind with silk ribbon, holding it in place with bugle beads.

Felting fabrics together is a simple and easy way to create an original base fabric for embellishment and stitch. The more fabrics you use, the more exciting the surface becomes. Quilting over the felting surface makes it pop and stand off from the fabric.

With foils, stitch, and sheer fabrics, a simple piece of velvet can be transformed into something luscious, 13" W x 5" L (33cm x 13cm).

Exploring Velvet: A MIXED-MEDIA PIECE
Angie Hughes

Over the past year or so I've been experimenting with the surface properties of cotton velvet. You can achieve some lovely quilted results creating a velvet, foil, and organza sandwich. The soft surface of the quilted velvet emulates the dewy, misty quality of a verdant garden—just the atmosphere I am trying to convey in my work.

I am inspired by plant forms and the paintings of Gustav Klimt, and you can see these influences echoed in the samples I have made for this project.

Techniques to Try

Materials

- White or pale-colored cotton velvet (or black cotton velvet for the Klimt samples)
  Note: I use cotton velvet because it can take all the repeated ironing that you must do for this project yet still yield that velvet look.
- Fusible interfacing
- 1" (3cm) foam brushes
- Flat palette
- Dye-na-Flow inks heat fixable
- Procion dyes or Brusho

- Good quality thickened bleach such as that from a Clorox Bleach Pen
- Acrylic paint
- Vinegar and water 1:1 solution in a spray bottle
- Absorbent kitchen paper
- A selection of (heat transferable) foils, sometimes called "transfoils"
- Organza
- Foil chocolate wrappers
- Small pieces of bright-colored silk fabric
- Metallic and colored embroidery threads
- Transparent colored organza
- Fusible webbing
- Baking parchment
- Sewing machine and threads
- Free-motion embroidery foot or darning foot
- Iron and ironing pad
- Basic sewing kit
- Heat gun (optional)
- Printing blocks, Indian wooden blocks, handmade string blocks

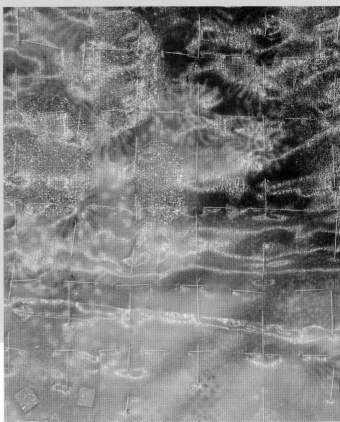

Velvet in this sample has been both painted and dyed.

DIRECTIONS

Painting the Background

STEP 1: Decide how big you want your piece to be, then iron your fusible interfacing to the back of your velvet. This will help to stabilize the fabric for free machine embroidery later on.

STEP 2: Paint your velvet with water so that the color will blend and blur. Paint on Dye-na-Flow color. I mix a couple of colors; my favorite is fluorescent pink at the moment. Dye-na-Flow fixes permanently when steamed. Steam iron to fix.

STEP 3: Paint again with water, then paint over with Procion dye mixed with water to add more color in washed out areas. For the water and Procion dye mixture, add enough Procion to the water to get the saturation of color you'd like to achieve; it's a personal preference. Make sure to completely dissolve the dye crystals in the water first before you paint. Leave the piece to dry.

STEP 4: Prepare an area with good ventilation or wear a mask when using bleach. Using printing blocks and stencils discharges the colored surface with thickened bleach. I use a sponge to apply the bleach to the block because you get a misprint, which gives the surface more character. When finished, spray with a dilution of vinegar and water to neutralize the bleach. Blot with a paper towel and leave to dry.

STEP 5: Add more texture and interest by sponging acrylic paints onto print blocks, then stamp onto the fabric. You should have an interesting multilayered background to which you can now apply foils and additional fabrics.

Working with Foils

We are using two types of foils in this sample—fabric foils (also sometimes called "transfoils") and foils from chocolate wrappers—and they are applied using two distinct techniques.

Foils from Chocolate Wrappers

Check that a foil really is metallic by tearing it; it will rip easily if it's aluminum. There are plastic foils on the market and you do not want to use them. Plastic foils melt nastily if you decide to zap the organza at a later step.

STEP 1: Cut fusible webbing to the size of the foil wrapper and iron it to the back of the wrapper.

STEP 2: Pull off the release paper, and iron the foil wrapper to the velvet surface. Think of the foil as a piece of fabric you would fuse by applying fusible webbing to the back of the material, iron to fix, remove the release paper, wrapper, and then fuse the wrapper to the fabric. Make sure the iron is on medium heat. You can cook fusible webbing if the iron is too hot.

~tips~

❖ To create specific shapes, cut shapes out of fusible webbing so that foil goes only in that area. Apply the fusible webbing as described.

❖ You can use the discarded release paper from the fusible webbing (essentially silicone parchment) as a mask to cut shapes and lay them onto the fusible. This way the foil only attaches to the exposed area of glue. Then remove the paper shapes and foil again with a different color.

❖ Using the nose of an iron, blend colors together on the fusible webbing by drawing with it through the foil onto the fusible web.

❖ You can mix the two different types of foils together (chocolate foil wrapper over the top of transfoil). When stitched, the effects are lovely.

In this working sample, squares and Xs of foil have been fused to the surface.

Transfer Foil

This is a heat-transferable foil traditionally used by card crafters and now used by textile artists.

STEP 1: Apply the fusible webbing to the surface of the velvet (rather than the foil) for this technique. Make sure that the fusible webbing is well attached to the surface of the velvet, and iron several times if you're not sure.

STEP 2: Lay the foil onto the fusible webbing, then place a piece of baking parchment on top to protect your iron, and in one firm stroke, iron with the heat on the medium setting.

STEP 3: Allow to cool completely. This is important, as you can sometimes pull the fusible webbing off the fragile velvet surface.

MACHINE EMBROIDERY

STEP 1: When you think you have enough detail on your piece, cover the surface with a piece of polyester transparent organza. This will prevent the stitches from sinking into the pile of the velvet. There is some nice shot organza around these days that is really affordable. Make sure that it is polyester if you want to melt the surface away with a heat gun for a more distressed look.

NOTE: Crystal organza is a bit difficult to see through when you're stitching, so I prefer the more transparent types. Pin then tack stitch over the surface to hold it in place and prevent the velvet from "creeping" the organza when you're machining.

STEP 2: Set your sewing machine for free-motion stitching.

STEP 3: I usually begin by outlining significant shapes with gold thread, but you could use any color. As you are working, remember that dense stitching will mask the velvet, so if you want to zap the surface with a heat gun, you need to leave areas of velvet exposed to later burn away.

~tips~

🐚 Try using vermicelli stitch for filling areas. This is a kind of wiggly stitch favored by quilters; the trick is not to cross over the lines.

🐚 If you are aiming for a linear stitch, "drunken wiggle" is good—just stitch a wobbly straight line and twist now and then.

🐚 One of my favorite stitches is the corded whipstitch, which involves loosening the bobbin tension and tightening the top tension slightly. This way the bobbin thread pulls up and covers the top thread, giving a delicate "satiny" stitch.

🐚 Keep your color palette simple, as it's quite a busy surface. Don't go over the top with too many colors. I find black thread really enhances some of the pattern with a simple outline.

FINISHING TOUCHES

When you have stitched enough, pin your piece onto a board and melt the organza with a heat gun. You could also just cut away areas if you prefer, or use a soldering iron. The heat from the heat gun will fracture the fusible webbing and change the foil surface a bit—a nice effect if you want an aged look. Hopefully, you will have a lovely sample to frame or inspire you to experiment further.

Machine embroidery is completed, and once the edges are bound or stitched, this piece will be ready for framing or to be made into a journal cover.

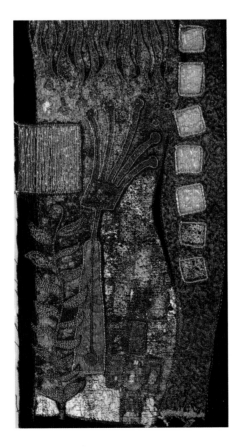

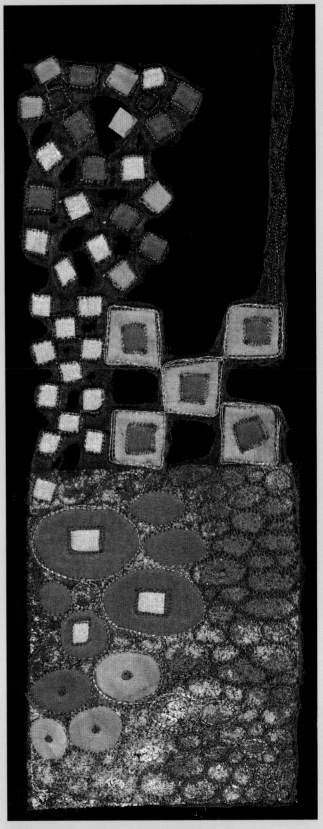

Machine embroidery is used to accent the shapes and integrate the different elements.

"Autumn Splendor," 12" W x 14" L (31cm x 36cm).

Dimensional and Embellished Appliqué
Heidi Lund

IF YOU'D LIKE TO ADD DIMENSIONAL APPLIQUÉS to your quilts, such as three-dimensional leaves, look no further. The methods shown here can be adapted to create a variety of structures to add to your quilts.

Techniques to Try

When it comes to leaves, do you need a little creative incentive and inspiration? Just pick up a book from the library about foliage, forests, or flowers. Or try my favorite activity, which is to go to a botanical garden and take your digital camera. Take photos of leaves and remember to turn leaves upside down and photograph the underside with veins. Use these pictures as inspiration for your art quilt and always remember that in nature no two leaves are made alike, so let your creativity bloom! I start out by designing my background fabric first and then set it aside to make all of my leaf components from various sources.

Materials

- ½ yd (½ m) of background fabric
- ½ yd (½ m) of cotton batting
- 3 fat quarters of silk dupioni (green, gold, and copper were used in this project)
- 3 fat quarters of satin or taffeta (green, gold, and copper were used in this project)
- Sulky Totally Stable stabilizer
- Sulky Fabri-Solvy water-soluble stabilizer
- Sulky Blendables Cotton variegated thread in 12 weight and 30 weight (color-coordinated to fabric)
- Sulky 40 weight variegated rayon thread (color coordinated to fabric)
- Steam-a-Seam2 Lite fusible webbing
- Silamide thread
- 90/14 topstitch needle
- 70/11 embroidery needle or quilting needle
- 7" (18cm) spring embroidery hoop
- Fibers in coordinating colors to match or "pop" from background and leaf shades
- Embellishments (beads, buttons, and charms)

Batik fabric has been stamped with gold Lumiere paint and free-motion quilted.

DIRECTIONS

STEP 1: Pick a background for your quilt of a favorite hand-dyed fabric or a batik that sings to your creative self. You can piece a background if you like, but I find myself using a special fabric that I was hanging on to, to "feature" in art. Choose to use the colors found in nature or venture out into your use blues, pinks, purples and reds. Work toward a finished size piece of approximately 14" x 14" (36cm x 36cm) or 12" x 18" (31cm x 46cm).

STEP 2: Cut a piece of cotton batting and quilt backing fabric the same size as your top piece. Set aside.

STEP 3: Use a leaf stencil or stamp to add surface design to your front background piece. After stamping or stenciling, set background aside to dry.

STEP 4: Once the paint is dry, fold the fabric and lay it on a cookie sheet or a flat aluminum pan and put into the oven at 170°F for 15 minutes to heat set your painted fabric. Your fabric is now safe for washing.

STEP 5: Take your background fabric and sandwich it with your batting. Turn everything over and iron Sulky Totally Stable stabilizer to the back of the batting. This stabilizer will keep your art quilt flat even after all the free-motion work, and you will leave it in your quilt permanently.

Tools and supplies I use to create my leaves. You'll notice I use a wide variety of hand and machine threads—everything from DMC hand threads to spools of variegated machine threads.

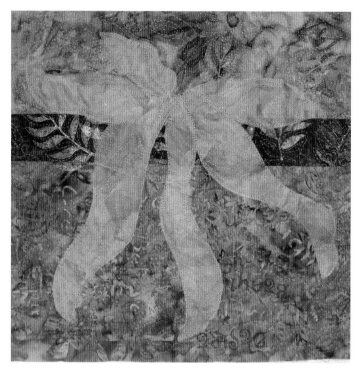

Quilt background, an example of piecing a background before embellishment.

Cotton thread and the top of your machine with 12 weight Sulky Blendables Cotton. Straight stitch around your leaf shape then go back over the straight stitching with a 2 to 2.5 free-motion zigzag.

STEP 3: Cut out leaves with sharp scissors, being careful not to cut into your free-motion stitches. Remember that no two leaves in nature are exactly alike. Give yourself the freedom to design a leaf shape of your own. As long as you can stitch it and cut it out it, it will work for this process. Set your fabric leaves aside.

Thread Leaves

Take a piece of organza or tulle and lay a piece of Sulky Fabri-Solvy over the top. Draw your leaf shapes onto the Fabri-Solvy. Using a 7" (18cm) spring embroidery hoop, hoop your design up and free-motion stitch on your sewing machine while it is still loaded with the Sulky Blendables Cotton thread. Cut out your sheer leaves, soak them in hot water to remove the stabilizer, and set them aside on a paper towel to dry. The cotton thread shrinks up a little bit and likes to curl, which gives the thread leaves a wonderful shape.

Background Stitching

Set your machine up with a 90/14 topstitch needle. For those comfortable with free-motion stitching, go ahead and free-motion your front background piece. Remember that this is an art quilt, so let you imagination guide you, and let your needle be your paintbrush. Design leaves, vines, flowers, circles, flames, or even just squiggles. If you are not comfortable with free-motion stitching, use one stitch or a combination of decorative stitches from your sewing machine on the background. Once the stitching is complete, you are ready to start making your leaf components.

Fabric Leaves

STEP 1: Take your fusible webbing and sandwich it between a layer of silk dupioni and a layer of taffeta or satin. Dupioni will be the top of your leaf, while the satin or taffeta will be the back of the leaf. Fuse the fabrics together with a hot iron. Be sure to iron both sides of the fabric to smooth out any wrinkles. If you are comfortable with drawing a leaf free-motion on your sewing machine, do that. If you're not comfortable, use a leaf template found either on a stencil or clip art program, or in your yard. Using a fabric marker or chalk pencil, trace around the leaf directly onto your fabric or make your own stencil using stencil paper or a file folder for shape.

NOTE: You can also use cotton, twill, polyester, upholstery, and suede fabrics for these leaves.

STEP 2: Set your machine up for free-motion stitching by dropping the feed dogs if possible and setting the tension according to the manufacturer's recommended settings. You will leave your machine in free-motion mode until you are ready to put on the backing fabric and binding. Load a 90/14 topstitch or quilting needle into your machine. Fill a bobbin with the 30 weight Sulky Blendables

Samples of the different leaves that can be created using taffetas and silk dupionis.

Dimensional Quilt Assembly

It is now time to decide if you would like to center your leaves or couch some fibers across your background piece to act as branches. Gather your leaves in groupings, lay the leaves in place, and tack them down with your sewing machine. Take a few fibers and wrap them around three or four fingers. Slide the wrapping off of your fingers, twist it in the center, and tack it down at the top of the leaves with your sewing machine. Once the fibers are tacked in place, go back and cut the loops and fluff up the fibers. You now have a distinct area to add embellishments.

Adding Embellishments

Here is where the handwork comes in. Using Silamide beading thread, a short beading needle, a thimble, and needle grabber, I add the embellishments. You can coordinate buttons, beads, shells, twigs, dyed silk carrier rods, silk cocoons, or other embellishments. I've added copper wire mesh leaves embossed with a metal embossing tool or beaded pictures from the floral section of my local craft store. Your leaf art quilt is your creation, so let yourself be free to add whatever you like.

NOTE: Silamide thread is a very strong nylon beading thread and holds up to extended use. A needle grabber looks like a small version of those rubber jar lid openers and is needed to help pull your needle through all the layers of fabric and fiber. A thimble is also useful to save your fingers!

Finishing Touches

After all of your embellishment is complete, there are multiple ways you can choose to add a quilt back to finish your art quilt. For example:

1. Sandwich your backing fabric behind your quilt and zigzag stitch around the edge to complete it.

2. Sandwich your backing fabric behind your quilt and add a traditional quilt binding.

3. Sandwich your backing fabric to the rear of your quilt and place a fused binding around the edge using a contrasting fabric and Steam-A-Seam2 Lite.

4. Place your backing fabric right sides together over the top of your quilt and stitch completely around the outside, leaving a small opening to turn your quilt out. Turn your quilt, whipstitch the opening closed, and whipstitch a few fibers twisted together around the edge if you choose.

Leaves free-motion stitched on a sandwich of silk dupioni, fusible webbing, and taffeta.

Thread leaves created on a stabilizer.

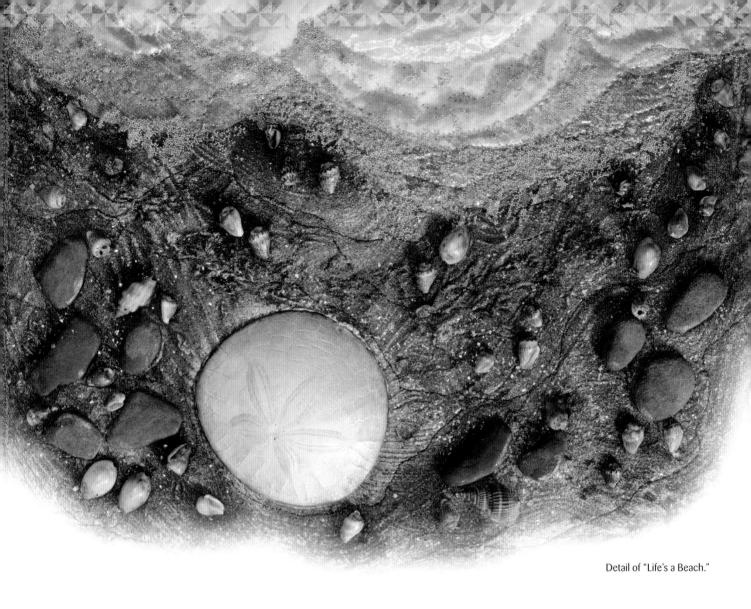

Expand Your Repertoire with Puff Paints
Linda S. Schmidt

ABOUT A YEAR AGO, my Scottish friend Carol Anne Clasper sent me a jar of Xpandaprint. This is a thick, glossy paint when wet, but when dried and puffed up by a heat gun, it becomes matte and three-dimensional. A variety of "puffy" paint products are available; be sure to choose the one that expands/puffs when heated. I almost discounted Xpandaprint entirely; however, having an inquiring mind, I experimented with it and found it to be an amazing medium with which to make art quilts.

Xpandaprint has many useful characteristics beyond puffing up. You can paint shapes and make indentations in it, rubberstamp with it, and also use it as very strong glue. It will secure anything you stick in it quite firmly. If you heat it with an iron or heat gun, it puffs up and creates a flexible, textured surface that can be sewn through and used in wall hangings and garments. I have made trees, rocks, bridges, waves, cliffs, walls, pavements, columns, buildings, statues, and borders.

Most recently I used Xpandaprint to create an art piece I call "Life's a Beach." This project is something anybody can do. It takes no special skill, just a spirit of adventure. If you'd like to try this, follow along with me and create your own "Life's a Beach" art piece.

Techniques to Try

Materials

- 1 small piece of fabric: 8½" x 11" (22cm x 28cm) or 12" x 14" (31cm x 36cm), or whatever size you want your finished beach to be
- 1 hard plastic surface to tape the fabric on top of
- Approximately 2 oz. of cream-colored puff paint such as Xpandaprint, Setacolor Pâte Relief à Expanser Expandable Paint, Puff Paint by Jones Tones, or Puffy 3D Paint by Tulip

NOTE: Be sure it is the kind of paint that requires heat to puff it and is not "dimensional paint" that puffs on its own.

- Small old paintbrush or other fine, blunt instrument
- Fan brush
- Small rocks, shells, sand, pebbles, and one focal-point shell
- Heat gun (embossing tool)
- Fabric paint in browns and metallic gold (I used Pébéo Setacolor in this project.)
- Gold or bronze metallic thread for quilting
- Sewing machine with darning foot and the usual sewing supplies
- Clear invisible thread (.004 mm)
- Batting the size of the finished piece
- Binding fabric

OPTIONAL

- Perfect FX (PFX) mica flakes
- Gold or silver glitter
- Jacquard Pearl-Ex powders
- Shiva Paintstiks (gold)
- Liquid Beadz

"Statue," 8.5" W x 11" L (22cm x 28cm).

DIRECTIONS

Preparing the Surface

STEP 1: Start with a piece of fabric that you know you'll never use or a worn-out pillowcase. Tape it down to a portable, plastic surface.

STEP 2: Cover the whole piece of fabric with about ⅛" (.3cm) of some version of puff paint. Just squirt it out of the tube or paint it from the jar onto a piece of fabric that is the finished size of the piece you want. This quilt is approximately 14" x 12" (36cm x 31cm).

STEP 3: Decide where you want the waves to be coming from, then take a pencil or other fine, blunt instrument (the end of a paintbrush or a defunct marker or pen will do) and draw little bird tracks in the puff paint, some distance away from the wave, and brush in a few ripples in the paint with your fan brush.

NOTE: Wash the paintbrush right away or the paint will stick the bristles together.

STEP 4: Add some rocks and maybe a focal-point shell just beyond where the waves will be; it makes no sense to put rocks or other stuff under the waves where you won't see them and might quilt over them by mistake. I decided to have my wave come in from the top, as if I were standing in the sand, watching the waves come in at my feet, so I left the top part of the piece empty.

Puff paints helped Linda form the rocks at the base of her Journal Quilt, showing Seven Falls in Colorado Springs.

STEP 5: Add some shells, just sticking them down into the paint; the paint acts like a very strong glue. Stick the rocks and shells in wherever you want them, but be aware you are still going to have to quilt this, so leave some spaces where you can stitch.

STEP 6: Sprinkle some sand, mica flakes, and gold or silver glitter over the whole thing. All of it will be caught in the puff paint and stuck down thoroughly.

Expanding the Surface

Now it's time to puff up the paint. The method you use will vary depending on the brand of paint, so be sure to follow manufacturer's instructions.

If you use Xpandaprint, it should be cured immediately after painting or printing with it. You can cure it in a heated oven at 140°C to 150°C (280°F to 300°F) for four to five minutes or 170°C to 180°C (335°F to 350°F) for one to two minutes. Be sure your fabric can tolerate the heat before curing. If you want to have some real fun and watch it as it puffs up, hold a heat gun about 6" (15cm) above the fabric and maintain a slow and steady movement until the Xpandaprint is opaque and fully risen. The product instructions say you can also dry the surface with a hair dryer for ten seconds, then turn it facedown on parchment paper, but that won't work with this project, because all of the shells and rocks would fall off.

WARNING: Do not touch the surface of the puff paint with an iron at any time. The paint will stick to your iron and you will be very, very sorry.

If you use Puff Paint, Puffy Paint, or Expandable Paint, let it dry naturally and thoroughly (it sometimes takes several hours); if you try to dry it with a heat gun or hair dryer, it starts expanding in a really gruesome fashion and looks like some really nasty viral or bacterial growth. You can, however, speed up the drying process by turning a fan on it or letting it dry outside in the sunshine. Once the paint is thoroughly dry, which takes one to twelve hours, depending on its thickness and the airflow, you need to heat it to expand it.

There are several ways to puff up the paint, as described above, but if you use a heat gun you will get to watch it happen and that's half the fun. I should also mention that the various puff paint products expand at different rates. Pébéo Expanding Paint and Xpandaprint puff up more than the Jones Tones Puff Paint or Tulip Puffy Paint. This is not necessarily a good thing, because if you are trying to make a rock or a tree and it expands too much, it distorts the underlying fabric. And I know from experience that you cannot flatten it with an iron.

You will have to watch your paint carefully and halt the heating process as soon as you achieve the results you want (another reason to use the heat gun over other methods).

Painting and Altering the Surface

As you puff it up, the paint will lose its gloss. This is a good thing because now you can paint it whatever color you like.

STEP 1: Using some dark brown fabric paint (I used Setacolor velvet brown transparent paint, diluted 50/50 with water), paint over the entire surface, letting the dark paint sink into the depressions and marks you made earlier. Then take a paper towel and rub it lightly over the surface, so the dark brown stays just in the crannies.

STEP 2: Take a little gold metallic and maybe some sienna brown transparent paint and dab it here and there. While the paint is still wet, you can add some Jacquard Pearl-Ex powder to give it an extra gleam. Let it dry, then add some gold or copper Shiva metallic Paintstik or some more metallic paint powders on top of that. Let it dry.

STEP 3: If some of the elements you embedded in the Xpandaprint absorb the paint color, you will have to deal with that. At one point, the sand dollar absorbed the brown fabric paint when I painted the background. I had no success when I tried to blot or bleach the color, so after I let the paint dry, I painted over the sand dollar with opaque Setacolor titanium white paint, then with Perle transparent paint.

STEP 4: Now add waves flowing up onto the beach. To do this, take some white, transparent, or opalescent sheer fabrics (silk organza, sparkle organza, or opalescent organdy), and cut curvy shapes out of them. You can use a wood-burning tool to cut the pieces out, which seals and cuts the fabric at the same time, or you can hold the edges near a candle flame to seal them so they won't fray. If you use a candle flame, first put your candle in a pie tin filled with water so you can drop the fabric in it if it catches on fire. Do not hold the fabric in the flame; just hold it up near the flame, and the edges will seal nicely.

STEP 5: Lay the sheer fabrics on top of your beach, overlapping them to form a series of glistening waves. If you want to add some bubbly effect, turn your heat gun onto some tulle, opalescent organdy, or sparkle organza. When you heat these fabrics with a heat gun, they bubble and become perfect fabrics to add texture to your wall hanging. If you heat them too long, they will get holes in them, but that works just fine for this project.

Stitching the Quilt

STEP 1: When you're happy with your arrangement of sheers, thread your sewing machine with invisible thread in the needle and the bobbin (I use YLI invisible .004mm thread). Sew all of the edges of the sheers to the background, taking one tiny stitch in the background and one on the fabric to be appliquéd. Use a .1 stitch length and a .1 stitch width.

STEP 2: Layer it with batting and backing, and quilt through the piece, quilting down the waves and around the rocks. If need be, take off your darning foot to be able to quilt around the shells and rocks. Be careful not to get your fingers caught under the needle.

STEP 3: Once it is quilted, bind it. After quilting and binding, add the final touch: Liquid Beadz. These tiny silver beads come embedded in clear glue, so all you have to do is smear them onto the edges of the waves with a palette knife or butter knife.

As you can see, puff paints can add some wonderful dimension to your quilts. The key is to think about how puff paint can be used judiciously and effectively in your quilt design. Experiment with puff paint and keep your samples in a textile notebook for future reference. Have fun!

Xpandaprint was used on this dimensional quilt border.

Puff paint tips

❧ To make a tree, squeeze the puff paint onto fabric in the desired shape, let it dry, puff it up, then paint it with fabric paints or Shiva Paintstiks and Pearl-Ex powders to make it shine. When you lay the finished shape on the background, sew it in place with a tiny zigzag stitch using invisible thread.

❧ To make a border using rubber stamps, dip a rubber stamp into the puff paint, print it on your background fabric, drizzle it with glitter while wet, and let it dry. When dry, heat the border with a heat gun, paint it with fabric paints and/or Jacquard Pearl-Ex powders, and let it dry.

❧ To make brick walls, draw the bricks into the wet paint with a pencil, drizzle the paint with sand or mica flakes, and let it dry. Puff it up, paint it, and you have a wall.

❧ To make a statue or a bridge, draw the shape onto fabric, fill it in with puff paint, then make the marks of the grooves into the paint. Let it dry, puff it up, and paint it

"Mystic Medieval,"
12" W x 15" L
(31cm x 38cm).

Making Fabric from Paper

Beryl Taylor

SO, YOU'VE FOUND A GORGEOUS STASH of wrapping paper you would love to incorporate into a quilt or fabric design. Too bad a needle would ruin the paper if you stitched it, right? Wrong. Learn how to turn paper into "fabric" using a few simple steps and tools you can find at your local craft store.

Technique to Try

Making fabric paper is an evolving technique and changes with every batch produced. It is a fantastic background for either machine or hand embroidery. The slight variations produced from batch to batch contribute to the unique beauty of your overall piece. The finished paper consists of three layers, and the process for producing the paper is carried out in four stages.

Materials

- ◘ 1 sheet of light-colored, 100% cotton fabric cut to size
- ◘ Magazine clippings, photocopies, gift wrap, tissue paper, text, or other printed materials
- ◘ Torn strips of lens tissue or craft tissue paper
- ◘ Fabric dyes or liquid acrylics in your chosen color scheme
- ◘ PVA or white glue
- ◘ Water
- ◘ A large sheet of plastic

DIRECTIONS

STEP 1: Lay the fabric on the plastic sheet. This enables you to peel the finished paper from the work surface later without it sticking.

STEP 2: Mix the PVA or white glue with water; the more diluted the mixture, the softer the finished paper, the less diluted, the stiffer the finished paper **(Figure 1)**. Paint the entire piece of fabric with the glue solution and place the magazine clippings or other paper scraps onto the fabric in a way that complements your vision of the finished piece **(Figure 2)**. This might involve completely covering the fabric or leaving spaces between the paper scraps; it's your choice. You can repeat images, arrange them in a pattern, or space them randomly. Tap the paper down so that it fuses with the solution-covered fabric.

STEP 3: While the fabric and the papers are still wet, apply another coat of the diluted PVA or white glue on top of the collage. Embed the torn strips of tissue into the glue layer and press them into the fabric with a sponge in order to remove any air pockets.

STEP 4: While the collage is still wet, paint it with the colored dyes or paints using a sponge applicator and allowing the colors to run into and blend with one another **(Figure 3)**. Let dry overnight, remove the finished product from the plastic sheet, and you have a sheet of collaged fiber that looks and sews like fabric.

Making fabric paper is a wonderful activity to do outdoors in the summertime. Often I make yards of fabric paper on a large table in the backyard, and dry them outside in the sun. By making large batches of fabric paper in a single afternoon, I then have a stash of different colors of fabric paper ready for use in my next project.

Figure 1.

Figure 2.

Figure 3.

Chapter Five
SURFACE DESIGN TECHNIQUES

Fabric painting and dyeing are just the jumping-off points for many quilters who want to create beautiful, one-of-a-kind fabrics for their quilts. In this chapter, artists show you how easy and fun it can be to color and embellish cloth with a variety of tools—some of which you may already have lying around your house. After you experiment with the following surface design techniques, it's a good idea to paste swatches of your samples into a textile journal for future reference. Over the years I have acquired piles of textile notebooks, and I flip through them from time to time to refresh my memory on certain techniques.

Foiling on Fabric

Jane Dunnewold

SHIMMER, GLIMMER, GLITZ, AND SHINE—foils add all of these, as well as textural interest, to fabrics of all kinds. Shinier than metallic fabric paint, foils are perfect as light-generating accents on clothing, quilts, or one-of-a-kind unique lengths of cloth. And foiling techniques are easy to learn and master, once you know a few simple tricks.

Foils

Foils aren't really metal at all but a plastic surface that looks like metal and is bonded to clear cellophane; the cellophane is peeled away after the foil has been bonded to the fabric. Foils are available in a wide range of colors and patterns, including holographic and rainbow versions. Some are lighter weight than others, such as those designed to be used with photocopiers or laser printers and found in office supply stores, but don't let that deter you— these can also be used with fabric.

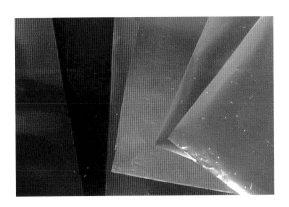

Silk screened foil.

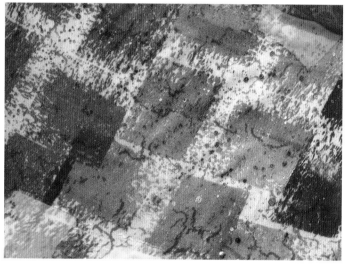

Stenciled foil.

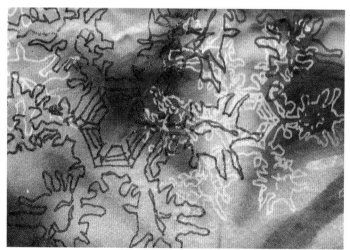

Silk screened foil.

Adhesives

Choosing the correct adhesive is critical to successful foiling. There are a variety of adhesives available. In general, an adhesive must meet two criteria in order to be appropriate for permanent foiling on fabric. First, the glue must be water-soluble. This means that while the glue is wet, water can be used to wash off both your tools and your fabric. (Just in case you make a mistake!) Solvent-based glues require paint thinners for clean up. This is hazardous to your health and can also be damaging to your tools. If in doubt about your adhesive choice, read the label. If the directions say water will remove the glue while it is still wet, you have the right product.

The second thing to consider is whether the glue will be permanent when dry. Water-soluble glues are like fabric paints—they can be cleaned up with water, but once dry, they are permanent. This is very important, as you want your foiling to stay put—especially if you are applying it to a surface you might clean often. Some glues are not meant to be used on fabric. Any glue that is considered an adhesive for paper, like Elmer's glue or Sobo glue, is not a good choice for foiling. Because the glue isn't permanent, as soon as the fabric gets wet, the foil will wash off.

Fabric

The fabric you choose to foil also plays a role in your success. Very smooth fabrics like silk charmeuse, China silk, rayon, and combed cotton are excellent choices for foiling because the smooth, even surface of the cloth will allow smooth and even foil application. If the surface is textured—like a silk noil or a heavy, rustic cotton—then the foil will be harder to apply, and a smooth surface will not be attainable. Fabrics should always be pre-washed before foil is applied. If you have previously dyed your fabric, or printed it with fabric paints, you should be sure the processes previously applied have been "stabilized" before proceeding with foiling. Stabilizing your fabric means removal of all excess dye, heat setting paints, and whatever else it takes to be sure your cloth won't bleed, fade, or lose paint after you've added the foil. Think of foiling as one of the final steps in your creative process. Foils will withstand some wear and tear, but they are not candidates for a dye bucket, and some paints won't stick to them when applied after the foiling has already been completed.

Applying Adhesives

Foiling adhesives are very similar to fabric paints in consistency, so they can be applied just like paint. Brush adhesive onto a stamp and then stamp it onto your fabric.

Or you can apply the glue through a stencil, using a flat stencil brush and an up-and-down motion. A small foam roller is another great way to apply adhesive using stencils. Just make sure the glue is evenly distributed on the roller in order to avoid printing some areas more densely than others. The adhesives are easy to silk-screen, and print beautifully through Thermofax screens. Handpainting is also an option. To ensure successful printing, size the scale of the lines or dots you want to make to the brush you choose. Heavy glue applications can change the hand of the fabric dramatically. Practice will help you to determine how much glue works best on any one fabric type, but in general less is better.

As you work with the various methods of applying the adhesive, you will notice the differences among them. Stamping, for example, prints the sheerest layer of glue on the fabric. The unique quality of the stamped image lies in its organic looseness, so choose stamping if you want texture or less-than-perfect images. Stenciling allows heavier glue application because you control how much adhesive you print based on how many times you pounce or roll through the stencil. Screen-printing allows for the most consistent and even foil applications of all methods, producing a foiled image that could be mistaken for a commercial print.

Adhesives should never be thinned with water. Doing so lessens the ability of the glue to hold the foil and leads to disappointing results. And never forget that the glue is always permanent when dry. If you don't like the images you have printed, you must wash them off immediately.

For Successful Foiling

* Fabric should be stabilized, clean, and dry. Iron fabric that is wrinkled, unless you want the wrinkles to become permanent.
* Apply glue by stamping, stenciling, handpainting, or screen-printing.
* Glue must be completely dry before the foil is applied. This can take an hour or more, based on how heavily the glue was applied.
* You MUST work on a hard, padded surface. An ironing board isn't usually strong enough to stand firm as you press. Use several layers of muslin on a countertop or table instead. Padding is needed, but the surface should not be soft.
* Set your iron to high. Most irons don't get hot enough to work well at the medium setting; if you have an expensive iron, you'll want to test whether it works best on medium or high.
* A Teflon surface is invaluable to this process. If your iron does not have a Teflon coating, you may need to use a pressing cloth. This can absorb heat and make it harder to attain results, so experiment.
* Work on small areas. It's harder to foil a big surface all at once. Work in sections.
* The cellophane layer is on the TOP. You are looking through it at the color. In order to keep this straight, use the foiling mantra: "See the color." It's easy to be confused and turn the foil color-side down thinking that it will peel off as color that way, but the cellophane keeps this from working. You must "see the color" in order to ensure the correct orientation of the foil sheet.
* Critical to the success of the foil application—USE THE SIDE OR TIP OF THE IRON. The foil glue softens if you spend too much time heating it, and you run the risk of melting the foil. Push the side or tip of the iron very hard, scuffing over the foil surface. Push away from your body as you count one, two, three. That should be long enough.
* Peel the cellophane back. If the area isn't foiled completely, you can reapply.

~tips~

❧ If you have tried to apply foil to an area several times unsuccessfully, add some fabric paint on top to disguise the adhesive because the glue may have sunk into the surface and the foil can no longer adhere properly.

❧ Experiment with different glues. Elmer's makes a fabric glue but it's too sticky to use on light fabrics unless you want to foil both sides. Aileen's Stretchable Flexible Fabric Glue is good, but dries clear and is hard to see on printed fabrics. Jones Tones makes a good adhesive, but it also dries clear and is expensive. Screen-Trans Development Company makes a gray adhesive. You can see it once dry, and it can be printed lightly enough that it doesn't change the hand of the fabric at all.

❧ Glue can be stamped, stenciled, or painted directly onto the back of the foil sheet, resulting in a very lightweight application, which is great for lighter fabrics.

❧ Fusibles can be used with foils. Lightweight fusibles are best, because the application doesn't change the hand of the fabric. Cut out your fusible shape, lay it on the fabric, and lay the foil over the fusible. When using fusibles, heat until you are sure the fusible is melted, but then let the cloth cool before you peel away the cellophane. The fusible glue is different from the liquid adhesive and if you try to peel away the foil while the surface is hot, the hot fusible will come with it.

"Sunflowers at Longwood Gardens," 19" W x 27" L (49cm x 69cm).

Painting
with Wax Pastels
Holly Knott

ARE THEY CRAYONS, watercolor pencils, wax pastels? Yes! And do they work on fabric? Yes! "They" are Caran d'Ache Neocolor II water-soluble wax pastels, which can be used to create wonderful surface design effects on fabric.

When these pastels are used with a lot of water, you can create diffused watercolor washes that are good for backgrounds. Used with little or no water, you can achieve more controlled and defined areas of color with sharper edges. Used alone, they can be used to draw areas of fine detail, shading, and sketchy pencil strokes on your fiber art pieces. These colors can be layered on top of each other as well.

The crayon-like consistency of Neocolor II pastels enables smooth application to both paper and fabric, and they're much softer than watercolor pencils. This is a plus when applying them to fabric because it lessens the "drag" that can cause fabric to stretch. You can draw directly on fabric with wax pastels and leave the effect "as is," or you can wet the surface with a paintbrush or spray bottle to dissolve the medium and create a more diffuse, painted effect. They must be heat set with a dry iron, using a pressing cloth.

Technique to Try

Materials
- Caran d'Ache Neocolor II water-soluble wax pastels
- White PFD (prepared for dyeing) fabric, or white muslin (prewashed)
- Masking tape
- Soft 2B (or similar) pencil
- Paintbrushes of various sizes
- Paper towels or extra piece of white fabric
- Iron
- Pressing cloth
- Work surface (I suggest foamcore or mat board covered with contact paper or thin plastic sheeting.)

DIRECTIONS
STEP 1: Cover a lightweight piece of foamcore, or foam board, with white contact paper or thin plastic sheeting to create a waterproof surface.

STEP 2: Cut a piece of PFD fabric slightly larger than the desired finished size, and, using masking tape, tape it to your work surface along the top edge only. Don't tape the sides or bottom, because the fabric may stretch some as it gets wet, and anchoring the top is really all you need to hold it in place.

STEP 3: Using a soft pencil, lightly sketch some of the key elements of your design onto the fabric.

STEP 4: Place a white paper towel under your fabric to absorb any excess water;

Caran d'Ache wax pastels were applied lightly to the fabric.

On the left side of the image only, a wet paintbrush was used to begin dissolving the pastels.

otherwise, the color will run too much. This step is critical if you want to maintain control of the bleeding when you begin to apply water. Be aware that if you leave the paper towel in place while the piece is drying, any texture on the paper towel may be visible on your painted creation (see the sky in "Sunflowers at Longwood Gardens" page 90). As an alternative, you could place another piece of white fabric under your design to see what interesting effects you get on it from the color that bleeds through. I've found that sometimes the entire image bleeds through, but in a paler version, which could be fun to incorporate into your creation or to use in an entirely different piece.

STEP 5: Once your design is complete, begin by lightly applying the Caran d'Ache pastels to the fabric, roughly filling in areas of color. The lighter you apply them, the paler the result you'll get when you wet the fabric. Leave some white space and be loose in your application; don't strive for perfection. Wetting the fabric will fill in the gaps. You can always apply more layers of color later, so don't worry if it seems too pale at first.

NOTE: If you use a lot of pressure, the color will go on darker, but the fabric may stretch a bit. I've found that holding a small area of fabric taut against the board with one hand helps keep it in place. In the sky shown here, I applied more blue with heavier pressure at the top so that it would be darker in that region.

STEP 6: Take a narrow paintbrush, dip it in water, wipe off the excess, and begin wetting your design by "painting" over it. The amount of water on your brush (as

well as the absorbing paper towel or second piece of white fabric underneath) will affect how much the pastels will run. You may have to brush over the same area a few times to completely dissolve the pastels. Remember to replace the paper towel or fabric underneath when it gets saturated if you don't want the colors to bleed further.

NOTE: A wider paintbrush is better for larger areas like the sky, working top to bottom in long strokes.

STEP 7: If some areas aren't dark enough after brushing the water onto the fabric, go back and apply more pastels. This can be done while the fabric is wet or dry.

NOTE: You can also dip the pastels in water and apply them to the fabric to create a softer line.

STEP 8: Using a dry Neocolor II pastel, you can sketch in lines to indicate shading (see the sunflower leaves). The pencil-drawing effect this dry application creates is unusual in a painted art quilt.

Heat Setting

When you're satisfied with your results, put a pressing cloth over your artwork and heat set it with a hot, dry iron. In my experiments, I have seen very little bleeding onto the pressing cloth.

I don't recommend washing the finished design, though.

A wet paintbrush was used over the entire image, dissolving all of the pastels. Then more color was added to various portions of the image to darken and enhance certain areas.

Threadwork

Any of your favorite quilting techniques can be applied to your finished creation. The hand of your fabric will still be very soft despite application of the pastels. In my quilts, I like to use matching rayon thread so it doesn't detract from the image itself, but you may want to use a contrasting or complementary color. I quilted around the edges of the petals, leaves, and stems to define their shapes. Then I added veins and did some meandering in the sky and background to rough-in clouds and the softer flower shapes in the more diffused areas. If your image bled a little more than you intended it to, don't worry—consider it a loose watercolor painting and your threadwork a pen-and-ink drawing on top of it. Remember, the color doesn't have to be contained within the stitching or outlines.

Pastels can also be used on fabric that was painted or dyed with other methods or they can even be used to enhance the color of commercial fabrics; you don't have to create an entire fabric painting. There is no limit to what you can do with Neocolor II water-soluble pastels. Experiment and have fun.

Leaf stencil made out of cardstock;
Shiva oil sticks on cotton.

Masking tape was used to make masked lines.

Shiva Paintstiks

Karen Williams

IF YOU'VE EVER TRIED PAINTING on dark fabric, you know that the hunt for the right paint is like the search for El Dorado. It is not easy to find a paint that remains bright and visible without changing the hand or feel of the fabric. Many fabric paints look best on lighter-colored fabrics and are simply too transparent to show up on a dark background. Others, like opaque acrylics, provide good coverage, but tend to stiffen the fabric and can be difficult to stitch through. So I felt like I'd discovered gold when I discovered oil sticks.

Oil sticks are professional-quality oil paints that have been solidified into an easy-to-use stick format. They can be rubbed directly onto the fabric, or can be used with stencils and masks for a variety of effects. You don't need a heavy application of the paint to get great color, and even with heavy application, the fabric is only slightly stiffer. Another plus is that once the paints have been cured properly and heat set, your piece is machine washable.

Oil sticks come in a wide range of colors, including one of the widest ranges of iridescent colors I have come across. I've found that the light- to mid-value colors and all of the iridescent colors

work wonderfully on dark fabrics. There are some exceptions (the darker blues, for instance) but there is a wide range of options. All colors of oil sticks work beautifully on lighter-colored fabrics.

My favorite brand is Shiva Professional Oil Paintstiks. These seem to have the highest pigment-to-binder ratio. If there is too much binder in an oil stick, you may see a waxy "bloom," or ring, around the edges of the painted area. This is more likely to happen with student-grade sticks because manufacturers use less pigment to make them less expensive.

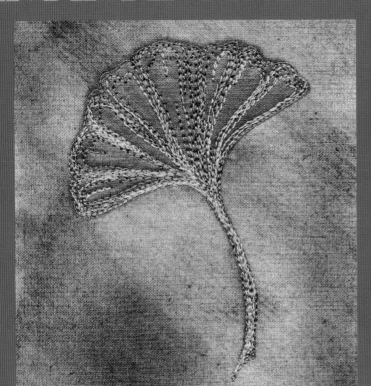

Stenciled leaf was free-motion stitched.

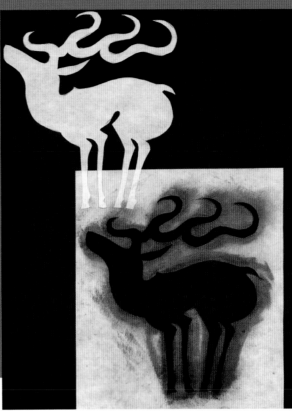

Sample reindeer stencil and mask made out of freezer paper.

Techniques to Try

Materials

- ▣ Oil stick paints
- ▣ Fabric to be painted
- ▣ Plastic to cover workspace
- ▣ Masking tape or painters' blue tape
- ▣ Card stock or freezer paper
- ▣ Craft knife
- ▣ Iron and ironing board
- ▣ Parchment paper
- ▣ Brush cleaner

OPTIONAL MATERIALS

- ▣ Synthropol or mild detergent
- ▣ Stencil brush or flat toothbrush

Preparing to Paint

I recommend covering your workspace with plastic when working with oil sticks, as the paint can be somewhat difficult to remove from some surfaces. I use a plastic drop cloth over my cutting table. It's important that the surface be smooth; any texture beneath will show up in your work as a result of the rubbing.

Unless you have purchased fabric labeled PFD (prepared for dyeing), you will want to prewash your fabric. Many commercial fabrics have finishes to repel dirt and prevent wrinkles, and these finishes can prevent the paint from bonding properly with the fabric. Prewash your fabric with Synthropol, a product made specifically for dyeing, or wash it with a mild detergent. Do not use fabric softener or dryer sheets; they will interfere with paint adhesion.

Tape your fabric to the cutting board, stretching it just slightly as you go. Either masking tape or painters' blue tape works well because it is not too sticky and can be removed cleanly later. This creates a stable canvas on which to work.

Using Stencils and Masks

Use masking tape to block out geometric shapes such as lines, squares, and triangles. Wherever you apply the tape, the fabric will keep its original color. You can paint between or inside of these masked lines. It is possible to create interesting compositions of positive and negative shapes this way.

Stencils work best for more complex shapes or organic shapes with curving lines. There are many commercially available stencils or you can make your own. Card stock and freezer paper both work well for handmade stencils. If your design is very detailed and you plan to use it only once or twice, I recommend freezer paper. The freezer paper stencil adheres to the fabric and helps prevent shifting of the complex design lines. For a simpler design or one you intend to use for multiple copies, use card stock, which is more durable.

Freezer Paper Stencil

DIRECTIONS

STEP 1: Draw your stencil design on the matte side of the freezer paper and carefully cut along the design lines with a craft knife. The finer the blade, the tighter the curves you will be able to cut. A craft knife is much more accurate than scissors. Keep in mind that you can use either the positive or negative shapes as a stencil or as a mask. For example, when I cut out my Siberian reindeer, I could use either the reindeer as a mask, or the outline of the reindeer as a stencil. It is simply a question of whether you want to color the shape or the background.

STEP 2: Once the stencil is cut out, iron the freezer paper, shiny side down, onto the right side of the fabric. This should be done on an ironing board, not on your plastic-covered work surface.

STEP 3: Allow the stencil and fabric to cool before you move them. The stencil seems to adhere more firmly that way. Then tape your fabric onto your work surface.

STEP 4: Card stock stencils are made and used in the same manner. Keep in mind that both sides of the card stock have a matte finish, so neither side will stick to the fabric. When using these stencils, you can simply hold them in place with one hand, or carefully tape them in place using masking tape.

✳ ✳ ✳

Stenciled reindeer.

Applying Color

The fastest way to paint with oil sticks is to work directly on the fabric. This will also give the heaviest coverage. Rubbing the oil stick on the fabric will give a rich, textured line with thick and thin areas of coverage. You can roughly fill an area with strokes of your oil stick (it's like working with a big crayon) and then use a stencil brush or flat toothbrush to produce a more even coverage or to blend colors. Scrub in small circular patterns with the brush. You can build up thick, solid layers of paint very quickly in this manner.

When applying paint through stencils, always start at the edge of the stencil and brush away from the edge. Consistently brushing into an edge can cause distortion. If you must brush into an edge, do it gently so that the stencil isn't disturbed.

Using Palettes and Mixing Colors

Applying paint to masking tape lines or to stencils can be tricky. I find using a palette keeps the paint where you want it, and keeps your stencils cleaner, which makes changing colors easier. For my palettes, I use freezer paper, cut into 3" x 5" (8cm x 13cm) squares. I work on the shiny side, because it is nonabsorbent and almost no paint adheres to the freezer paper. Paints blend and mix well on freezer paper. For a lighter effect reminiscent of airbrushing or a color wash, rub the paint onto a palette and then brush it from the palette onto the fabric.

You can designate a brush for each color, but I typically work with only three brushes—one each for yellows, blues, and reds. I brush the extra paint off onto plain printer paper, which can end up being a decorative work itself.

Shiva Paintstik color sampler.

Rub the paint onto the palette as if you are smearing lipstick. Then brush the paint off of the palette onto the fabric using long, smooth strokes. The paint will be the densest and brightest at the start of your stroke and will feather out and fade from there. Be forewarned that this technique can be deceiving. When you look at the fabric with the masking tape in place, the paint may seem quite faint, but when you remove the tape, the painted areas practically pop and are very visible. So you may want to check your progress as you work, gently lifting a section of the stencil or the mask.

You can mix colors by working wet-into-wet or by mixing them on the palette. Wet-into-wet simply refers to applying one color of oil stick immediately over another and then using a brush to blend them. The wet-into-wet method produces colors that are less fully blended; both the original colors and their blend will likely be visible. In a red and yellow mix, you'll see red, yellow, and various oranges. Mixing on the palette offers a more consistent blend—the same red and yellow mix will produce a more uniform shade of orange.

Another way to mix colors is to allow the paint to cure overnight and then continue painting. The cured paint will feel dry to the touch and the new paint will not physically blend with the paint that has cured. Thinly brushed layers of new color can create some wonderful transparent effects.

Finishing Up

I use a citrus-based automotive cleaner to clean my hands and brushes. Readily available at most hardware stores, it is a bio-degradable, less-toxic alternative to turpentine and other paint thinners. Squirt a quarter-size dollop into the palm of your hand or into a small container and swirl a brush in the cleanser. Treat each brush individually, adding another dollop of cleanser for each brush. Once all of the brushes have been treated, squeeze out another dollop and rub the cleanser over your hands. Finish with a warm-water rinse for both the brushes and your hands.

The paint must be cured in order to make the colors fast. To do this, place the fabric in a well-ventilated area for at least 48 hours; three days to a week is the actual recommendation. The paint can smell a little funny while it's curing. Once the paint has been properly cured, it's ready to be heat set. Sandwich the area to be set between two layers of parchment paper, then iron the fabric using a heat setting appropriate to the fiber content. After curing and heat setting, your piece is machine-washable. Turn the fabric inside out, if possible, and launder as usual. Use a low heat setting for the dryer or line dry. Do not dry-clean because the dry-cleaning solvents can cause the paint to run.

~tips~

❧ Between uses, a thin skin will form over the surface of your oil sticks. This is a result of oxidation. The surface layer of the oil stick reacts with the oxygen in the air, forming a skin. This skin prevents further oxidation and prevents the sticks from drying out. Before you can use the sticks, you will need to remove this skin. The easiest way is to scrub the oil stick on a piece of scrap paper. Most of the skin will flake off, although you may need to pick off some remaining flakes. You can also use a sharp craft knife to get under the skin and gently peel it away. This skin is very thin, so don't cut too deeply.

❧ Painting on fabric with oil sticks can add unexpected shine to your quilts and wearable art. Now that you're armed with the basic techniques, you have one of the essential tools to add to your surface design repertoire.

Stenciled reindeer with free-motion stitching.

"Old Growth,
New Growth,"
13" W x 20" L
(33cm x 51cm).

Discharge Discovery

Dina Buckey

DISCHARGING FABRIC IS SIMILAR to an archeological excavation: by removing the top dye, you uncover the hidden treasure of another color and discover a whole new world below. These hidden colors vary widely but usually range from tannish brown to reddish brown. The length of time the bleaching agent is left on the fabric will determine the value intensity of the underlying color.

Techniques to Try

Materials

- Chlorox Bleach Pen, Soft Scrub with Bleach, or another cleaning agent that contains bleach and has a gel-like consistency
- Heavy plastic drop cloth to protect your work surface
- Rubber gloves
- Respirator
- Hydrogen peroxide
- Measuring cups dedicated to bleach (used specifically to measure hydrogen peroxide)
- Two heavy plastic containers with a five-to-ten-gallon capacity (one for the peroxide/water mixture, the other for clear water)
- Foam paint roller with plastic paint tray
- Spray bottle filled with a solution of half water, half liquid bleach
- Crayola Super Brush with the flange-end attachment
- Mylar cutouts, stencils, waxed paper, saran wrap, and plastic Bubble Wrap
- Cotton, rayon, or linen fabrics in dark colors

CAUTION: It is important to work in a well-ventilated area when working with bleach. Wear a respirator, eye protection, and rubber gloves; bleach is a skin and eye irritant.

Preparing the Surface

STEP 1: Cover all work surfaces with plastic and wear old clothing or an apron. Do not use any containers or implements that you would use with food, as ingesting bleach can be fatal.

STEP 2: Start with small pieces of fabric no larger than 15" x 15" (38cm x 38cm). The second the bleach solution touches the fabric, it reacts; by working with smaller pieces, you are able to control the results.

STEP 3: Prepare one large plastic container with a solution of one part hydrogen peroxide to eight parts water. This is to neutralize the bleaching action.

STEP 4: Fill the other large plastic container with clear water. This is for the final rinse of the peroxide/water solution.

Neutralizing the Bleaching Action

It is important to neutralize the bleaching process, or the bleach can eat holes through the fabric. Prior to neutralizing, you must rinse off the excess bleach from the fabric. When rinsing off small pieces, simply swish the material under running water in a sink. When I discharge yardage outdoors, I use a garden hose.

DIRECTIONS

STEP 1: After rinsing off the excess bleach, place the fabric in the peroxide/water container. Allow it to sit for 5–10 minutes. If the fabric should soak for longer than 10 minutes, it will not hurt the fibers.

STEP 2: Remove the fabric from the peroxide/water mixture and gently squeeze out the excess water.

STEP 3: Put your fabric in the clear-water container and soak it for an additional 10 minutes.

NOTE: When I am doing multiple layers of discharging, such as with the double-discharge technique, I dry the fabric between each discharging process; you may either hang it to dry or use a clothes dryer.

Foam Stamp.

Bubble Wrap.

Foam Stamps

STEP 1: Dip foam stamp in Soft Scrub with Bleach.

STEP 2: Press it onto fabric, then carefully lift the stamp off.

STEP 3: In a sink, rinse the Soft Scrub from the fabric.

STEP 4: Neutralize the bleaching action as described above.

Bubble Wrap

STEP 1: Cut a piece of Bubble Wrap the same size as your fabric.

STEP 2: Using a foam brush, dip the brush in Soft Scrub and paint the top of the Bubble Wrap.

STEP 3: Press the Bubble Wrap, painted-side down, on the fabric, and then carefully lift it off. The bleach will react quickly and you will start to see circles appear on the surface almost immediately.

STEP 4: In a sink, rinse the Soft Scrub from the fabric.

STEP 5: Neutralize the bleaching action.

Waxed Paper

STEP 1: Crinkle waxed paper into a ball shape and dip the ball into Soft Scrub.

STEP 2: Remove the excess Soft Scrub by pouncing the waxed-paper ball on paper towels.

STEP 3: Randomly dab the fabric with the waxed-paper ball.

STEP 4: Reload the ball with Soft Scrub, if needed, and repeat.

STEP 5: Rinse the fabric to remove the Soft Scrub and then neutralize the bleach.

Ginkgo Leaf Cutouts

This technique from Colleen Wise started my love for discharging fabric.

STEP 1: Cut gingko leaf shapes out of Mylar or heavy plastic. Any kind of shape can be used, but make sure it is not too detailed.

STEP 2: Place the leaf shapes randomly on your fabric. In my ginkgo leaf wall hanging, I intentionally placed the Mylar shapes in a vertical formation to duplicate falling leaves.

STEP 3: Fill a spray bottle with a 50/50 solution of bleach and water; clearly mark the contents on the outside of the bottle.

STEP 4: Lightly spray the fabric with your bleach solution, being careful not to move the leaf shapes.

STEP 5: Carefully lift the plastic shapes off of the fabric.

STEP 6: Rinse and neutralize the fabric.

Crinkled waxed paper.

Mylar Ginko Leaf.

Crayola Super Brush

One day I saw a commercial for an outdoor toy that created starburst designs with washable paints. I knew I could duplicate the patterns on fabric using Soft Scrub with Bleach instead of paint, and it worked like a charm. This technique takes some practice, is messy, and you need to work quickly.

NOTE: When using this technique, I work with 1 to 2 yards (1 to 2 meters) of fabric laid out on the driveway because the bleach will splatter quite a distance.

STEP 1: Fill a medium-size plastic container with Soft Scrub; the Super Brush has an interior reservoir that will be filled from this container.

STEP 2: Lay large sheets of plastic on an outdoor area and lay your fabric yardage on top of the plastic. Tape the fabric in place if it is a windy day.

STEP 3: Fill the interior reservoir of the Super Brush with Soft Scrub; do not attach the flange end yet. To fill, immerse the bottom of the toy in Soft Scrub and pull the orange knob on the top toward you. You will see the interior fill with the white Soft Scrub.

STEP 4: Screw on the flange tip and slowly push the top orange knob down. When you see the Soft Scrub start to come out of the holes of the flange tip, stop pushing the orange knob down.

STEP 5: Position the Super Brush vertical to the fabric and quickly push down on the flange tip. You will see the Soft Scrub squirt out of the small holes around the bottom of the flange tip. The harder you push on the flange tip, the wider your starburst image will be.

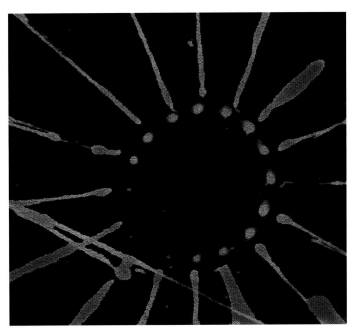

Crayola Super Brush.

Double-discharge.

NOTE: The reservoir chamber does not hold much Soft Scrub; you may need to keep refilling the chamber. Also, you will need to periodically push down on the orange knob on the top to keep the Soft Scrub in the flange end, otherwise nothing will come out.

CAUTION: Once you've used the Super Brush for discharge art with a bleach product, be sure to mark it clearly so that it will not be used as a toy.

Double-Discharge Technique

A very gifted friend of mine came up with this ingenious technique. She wanted to create depth in her discharged work and achieved this by overlapping previously discharged areas with new ones.

STEP 1: Fold a square or rectangular piece of fabric in half. Iron the middle to create a definite crease and then open the fabric flat.

STEP 2: On one side, squirt Soft Scrub in a random pattern. Fold the other side of the fabric over on top and lightly press down. You will begin to see the fabric being discharged on the wrong side.

STEP 3: After about 15–20 seconds, rinse off the Soft Scrub and then neutralize.

STEP 4: Dry the neutralized fabric completely and then repeat Steps 1 and 2. This time, leave the Soft Scrub on for 30–45 seconds and then rinse and neutralize. You will have a mirror image of your design on the other side, giving you an image wide open to interpretation.

Lines, Lettering, and Precision Graphics

Words, symbols, or precise graphics can all be achieved with the Clorox Bleach Pen. There are two ends to the pen; I use the end that has the fine tip to write words, numbers, and other precise images. Gently shake the bleach pen, unscrew the cap, and write on your fabric. Maintain a gentle pressure on the middle of the pen to allow a continuous flow of bleach.

Tile Impressions

Working on top of a mosaic tile surface or other irregularly shaped flat surface can result in interesting patterns, but be careful to work on a surface that will not be discolored or damaged by the bleach. One day I had some friends over to play, and my friend Joan accidentally left some Soft Scrub on my outdoor mosaic table and placed her black rayon fabric on top. This accident resulted in the tile pattern of the table discharging onto the fabric with an interesting effect.

STEP 1: Place rayon or lightweight dark fabric over a mosaic or other flat, fragmented surface.

STEP 2: Squirt Soft Scrub into a plastic tray designed for a paint roller.

STEP 3: Load a foam paint roller with the Soft Scrub, making sure the entire roller is thinly and evenly coated.

STEP 4: Roll the paint roller over the fabric with firm, even pressure. You will begin to see the image of the tiles come through the surface of the fabric.

NOTE: The fabric will tend to want to move on you, so keep smoothing the fabric out and work in small sections at a time.

Once you've experimented with discharging fabric, you'll never look at your bottle of Soft Scrub or other bleach product the same way again! Discovering the hidden color beneath by discharging fabrics is an exciting process, and the resulting fabrics can turn out rather beautifully.

"Ginkgo Leaves," 20" W x 30" L (51cm x 76cm).

"Two Sunflowers,"
12" x 12"
(31cm x 31cm).

Layered Printmaking

Lucie Summers

ONE DAY, DURING ONE OF MY RARE URGES to tidy up, I came across a battered box full of some of my old projects from art college. At the bottom of the box was a piece of work I had done years ago and had completely forgotten about. It was a lino-printed piece, printed, cut, and reassembled in rusts, pinks, and browns, and it immediately recaptured my interest. This layered piece became the starting point for a quilt that I made for an exhibition.

Rediscovering this old piece of art offered me a great chance to use a color palette I don't use very often. I then became interested in recreating the same printing technique, layering, for other pieces. Since then, I have often used this method to produce series of small quilts (around 12" [31cm] square). This method also produces interesting results when used in larger pieces in conjunction with other techniques.

With a bit of preparation, it is easy and quick to produce really good results with layering. I managed to create several examples on the kitchen table while simultaneously entertaining a grumpy, teething one-year-old, watching an old episode of *Diagnosis Murder* on TV, and whipping up a three-course meal for four. If you spend a few hours printing lots of images, you can stockpile them for use in many other projects such as bags and book covers.

Print Blocks

I usually use lino to create my own print blocks. It is rather time-consuming to cut, but produces a very durable block that can be used over and over. I also make two blocks of the same image, one positive, and one negative. I feel it gives the work greater depth and more interest. It is not necessary to cut your blocks from lino; as an alternative they can be made using funky foam stuck onto a cardboard or wood backing.

The following information is only a guideline; there are no hard-and-fast rules. Please feel free to experiment.

Techniques to Try

Materials

- ◻ 1 large print block (or more) made from lino or any other material
- ◻ Lino-cutting tool and blades (if cutting your own block from lino)
- ◻ Acrylic craft paints (3 to 4 colors)
- ◻ Pébéo Setacolor Transparent Paint, or Jacquard Textile Color in two to three colors (or any product suitable for "glazing")
- ◻ Base fabric: Enough to print at least two to three images next to each other. (Cotton curtain lining fabric soaks up color well and frays nicely.)
- ◻ Top fabric (three to four pieces)
- ◻ Craft knife, cutting mat, and ruler
- ◻ Large paintbrush
- ◻ Foam rollers
- ◻ 505 Spray and Fix for basting
- ◻ Iron
- ◻ Sewing machine with walking foot
- ◻ Threads to match fabrics (cotton or rayon)
- ◻ Square of thin polyester batting
- ◻ Piece of cotton for backing
- ◻ Threads of various thicknesses for embellishment

OPTIONAL MATERIALS
- ◻ Large rubber roller
- ◻ Carbon paper sheet
- ◻ Sharp pencil
- ◻ Access to photocopier
- ◻ Beads and sequins for embellishment

Example of cut lino block.

"Four Sunflowers,"
12" x 12" (31cm x 31cm).

Positive Images

STEP 1: Decide on your block size. As a guide, the leaf blocks shown here measure 4" x 12" (10cm x 31cm), while the sunflower blocks are 6" x 12" (15cm x 31cm). These are both good sizes to work with because they fit nicely into 12" (31cm) squares.

STEP 2: Cut your lino to the desired size. You can use a craft knife on a cutting mat for this.

STEP 3: Using a pencil, draw your design on the lino. Remember that your design will be printed in reverse onto the fabric. Decide which pieces you wish to remove and scribble over them to remind yourself which bits to cut.

STEP 4: Using the lino-cutting tool with a sharp V-shaped blade, cut around the outline of the design, always cutting away from yourself. You may find it useful to keep a warm iron next to you while cutting the block. Ironing over the top of the lino from time to time warms the surface and makes it very easy to cut.

STEP 5: Cut out the rest of the design using the different-shaped lino cutting blades as necessary.

Negative Images

STEP 1: To make a "negative" block, make a photocopy of your finished "positive" lino block.

STEP 2: Place a piece of carbon paper ink-side down on top of a new piece of lino, then place the photocopy on top facing upward.

STEP 3: Using a sharp pencil, draw around the design as accurately as possible. Scribble over the new pieces you wish to cut. These should be the bits that are solid on your first block. Anything that was cut away on your first block should be left in place on this block.

STEP 4: As before, cut the block using the lino-cutting tool.

STEP 5: Make sure you are happy with the results by printing both blocks with acrylic paint onto a piece of scrap paper or fabric.

Preparing the Fabric

Decide on your color scheme. If you do not wish to use a plain fabric (which works very nicely if you don't want to color your own) for the base, consider using hand-dyed, handpainted, or commercially printed fabric. Fabrics with subtle shifts in color, such as marbled or variegated fabrics, also work quite nicely. The toning top fabrics can be a variety of weights. Try plain brushed cotton or felt as well as craft-weight cotton or silk. Don't buy anything especially for this project; use whatever you have on hand. If the colors are not quite right, this can be remedied with a wash of Pébéo Setacolor Transparent or Jacquard Textile Color.

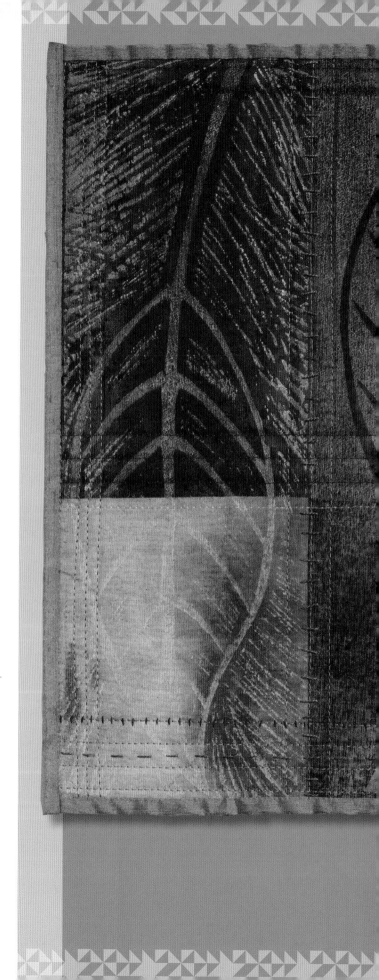

"Red Skeleton Leaves," 12" x 12" (31cm x 31cm).

Printing the Fabric

STEP 1: Begin by printing the block onto the base fabric using different colors of acrylic paint. If using 2 blocks, alternate them.

STEP 2: Print the top fabrics in the same way using a variety of different colors.

STEP 3: If any of your prints are too pale, use a large brush to paint a strong wash of Pébéo Setacolor Transparent or Textile Color over the background to tone it. The acrylic paint acts almost like a resist (I say "almost" because the acrylic paint does get lightly tinted), so the print should now stand out beautifully.

STEP 4: Let fabric dry, then iron.

STEP 5: Take the top fabrics and cut the excess from around each print. You don't need to leave a seam allowance.

STEP 6: Take a deep breath and cut through the images. Cut them horizontally or vertically; either works really well in this technique.

STEP 7: Place the cut pieces on top of the base fabric, matching up the prints like you are assembling a jigsaw puzzle. You may not need all of the pieces—put any extras aside for another project or print more base fabric to use them up.

STEP 8: When you are happy with the arrangement, use a basting spray to bond the top fabrics to the base.

STEP 9: Using a sewing machine, stitch over all of the raw edges. Try a satin stitch or running stitch. Running stitch is particularly nice if you have a lovely raw edge to show off.

STEP 10: Layer up the base fabric with the batting and the backing fabric using the basting spray.

STEP 11: Using a different color thread, fit your machine with the walking foot and quilt a random grid in straight lines over the entire piece. I usually use 3 colors when quilting—2 that blend and one that contrasts.

STEP 12: After quilting, give the quilt a good press with a hot iron—I prefer a really flat appearance to my work.

STEP 13: Bind your work with a ¼" (.6cm) binding.

STEP 14: At this stage, add any embellishments you wish. Rows of iridescent bugle beads following the quilting lines look gorgeous, as do lines of running stitch. Layer up different sizes and shapes of sequins and top off with a seed bead. Try clusters of French knots and seed stitching.

Once you're happy with your masterpiece, stand back and admire!

~tips~

☙ Exercise some caution if you decide to cut both horizontally and vertically in the same piece of work as it can look rather busy. Remember, simplicity is the key.

☙ Take your time with the composition.

☙ If you are unhappy with any of the colors, recolor them with Pébéo Setacolor Transparent or Textile Color. My "Red Skeleton Leaves" piece was awful until I drenched the background with richer colors.

Mercerized cotton broadcloth; dyed, bleach-resist monoprinted, overdyed, freezer-paper resist.

Cut from Your Imagination:
RESIST-PRINTING FABRIC WITH PAPER SNOWFLAKES
Melanie Testa

I BEGAN QUILTING at the age of nineteen and promptly fell head over heels for fabric, especially hidden conversational prints. Salvatore Ferragamo neckties are the ultimate example in this genre. What looks like a predictable and orderly design from afar, upon closer inspection reveals tiny tigers hiding behind bushes preparing to pounce, while simultaneously looking cute and lovable. These ties make you lean in to the wearer to see what is going on, in effect encouraging you to have a conversation about them.

I love fun motifs that pop off the cloth and make you smile, but you don't have to be a famous designer to create them. You can achieve the same effect using fabric paint and freezer-paper "snowflakes" cut into fun shapes like birds, trees, or rabbits.

The overall pattern will look uniform and geometric, but the "hidden" pictures will give your fabrics a touch of mystery and intrigue. This process involves a bit of preparation, but once you have all the tools in place, the technique is fast, easy, and fun.

Technique to Try

Materials
- Pencil
- Reynolds brand 18"-wide (46cm) freezer paper, cut into 6" (15cm) squares and folded in quarters (16 to 20).
- Stapler
- Scissors and X-acto knife
- Cutting mat

Making Freezer Paper Patterns

STEP 1: Before you cut, be sure your pattern is original or taken from a book or CD of copyright-free patterns.

STEP 2: Making "snowflakes" or patterns is similar to making a stencil; you will need to leave a "bridge" that connects the cutout areas of your folded square. You do this by leaving an overlapping area on both of the folded edges of your folded freezer-paper squares. This will create a beautiful repeating pattern that mirrors itself in a radial fashion. (See diagram, right.)

STEP 3: Test out various placements of your design on the freezer-paper squares. Creating a pleasing design is what the technique is all about. When you feel the composition of your design is complete, cut the design out of a folded freezer-paper square and use this as a template for the remainder of the squares. To create a fat quarter of cloth you will need approximately 16–20 patterns.

STEP 4: Carefully staple the layers in place to prevent shifting and to facilitate cutting. Make sure to place the staples outside of your design; otherwise, paint will seep into the holes left after the staples have been removed.

STEP 5: Cut fussy areas first, while the staples are securing the layers together. You may need to use an X-acto knife to cut out areas that are difficult to get to. Cut the outside edges last. Store your patterns flat until you are ready to use them.

✳✳✳

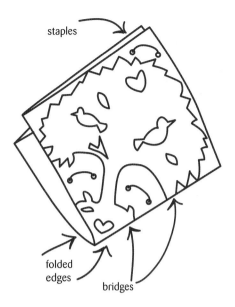

staples

folded edges

bridges

Get Ready to Paint

Here comes the fun part! Now that you have created your stencils, you are ready to paint. I suggest since you'll be working with fabric and metallic paints that you don an old t-shirt or apron to protect your clothing (just in case).

~tip~

☙ Make several copies of your original drawing so that if you make a mistake you have another copy available. Starting simply, with patterns created from hearts, flowers, or stars, will take some of the guesswork out of the entire process and allow more time for experimentation.

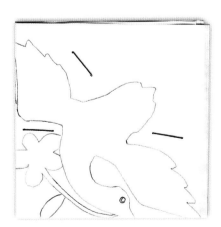

This image was traced onto the freezer-paper square and stapled.

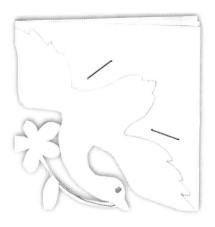

The traced image was cut carefully so that the "bridges" were left as needed.

Finished snowflake.

Mercerized cotton broadcloth; discharge stamped, stamped, freezer-paper resist.

Materials

- Several fat quarters
- Studio Basics, non-latex, round, blending cosmetic sponges
- 2"-wide (5cm) masking tape
- Jacquard Neopaque and Lumiere paints
- Bucket of water
- Palette (such as a piece of Plexiglas) or a plate
- Iron and ironing cloth
- Scrap cloth

DIRECTIONS

Prepare all fabric by ironing and laying flat. Wrinkles will be accentuated in this technique, so iron your cloth thoroughly. Make the daubers to apply paint. You can use sea sponges for this, but I prefer cosmetic sponges as they are made of high-density foam and, when used properly, can give you a gentle, airbrushed effect.

Making the Dauber

STEP 1: Begin by ripping several 5" (13cm)-long strips of masking tape and putting them aside.

STEP 2: Gather up the outside edge of a round cosmetic sponge in your hand (**Figure 1**) and wrap the edge, about ⅜" (1cm) from the bottom, with a piece of the precut tape (**Figure 2**). Crush the remaining tape to itself, making a little handle (**Figure 3**). Make sure the sponge creates a nice round "dome" shape.

~tips~

&ce; When mixing paints to cover areas of your base fabric, you will need to mix colors of the same value and darker. I recommend starting out with fabrics that are light to medium in value.

&ce; When mixing paints to color your cloth, a good place to start is in the analogous range (such as yellow, orange, and red). If your cloth is yellow, try working with orange, red, and brown tones.

&ce; Keep a piece of Plexiglas or a palette near your paints. This will enable you to mix paints quickly and with a sense of adventure—trust your judgment.

&ce; If you feel the need to wash out your sponge in order to change colors, press excess water out thoroughly before using it again; otherwise, water stains will occur while applying your next color. To be on the safe side, I recommend using a fresh, dry dauber rather than washing one you've already used.

Figure 1.

Figure 2.

Figure 3.

Mercerized cotton broadcloth; dyed, freezer-paper resist.

Make a Sample

If using a dauber is new to you, making a sample is very important. A sample will help you learn the amount of pressure needed to apply the paint and will also allow you to make mistakes without fear of ruining your good cloth. Using a dauber to pounce color takes a little practice. You are looking to create a gradation of color that emanates from the outer edge of your freezer-paper cutout and fades to nothing. Once you're comfortable with the dauber, you'll find you can control the amount of paint you apply by exerting more or less pressure. In this way, as you work, you can decide when a section of the fabric has reached saturation and then move on to another section.

DIRECTIONS

STEP 1: Iron a sample "snowflake" onto a scrap piece of cloth.

STEP 2: Apply paint evenly to your sponge. Do this by spiraling the sponge in place in the paint on your palette. Tap the sponge onto the palette and look at the surface of the sponge. Remove any pools of paint around the edges of the sponge. Pools will leave moon-shaped blotches on your cloth when you pounce. The paint should soak into the sponge evenly.

STEP 3: Begin daubing the paint over your secured cutout.

STEP 4: When your sponge is freshly loaded you will not need to apply much pressure to get an even layer of paint. As the amount of paint on the sponge decreases, you will need to use more pressure to apply the paint to the cloth. With practice you will be able to apply gradations from dark to light. Practice with your sample until you feel you have grasped the technique. Now you are ready to create the real thing.

The possibilities are endless; this process can be as simple or as involved as you like. You can overlap your cutouts, make geometric patterns, using one or several colors. The choice is yours. Just remember that there are no mistakes in art, just new creations, new pathways. Your results will be as unique as a snowflake.

"Sing It!," 4" W x 6" L (10cm x 15cm).

Preserving Poppies," 25" W x 31" L (64cm x 79cm).

Fiber Tiles:
WORKING WITH DIGITAL IMAGING FOR ART QUILTS
Julie Hirota

OVER THE YEARS, I'VE FILLED MY CREATIVE TOOLBOX with experiences in many areas. I've always been attracted and inspired by glass and ceramics and first became excited about creating "fiber tiles" when I saw a tile artist at an art show in northern California. Using my previous experiences in clay, photography, illustration, and digital manipulation, I incorporated these skills into my textile pieces to create a soft tile quilt. The fiber tile allows me to use many techniques while still taking the tactile approach of stitching. From a distance, and even close up, most of my clients are not convinced that my work is a textile until they actually touch it. A compliment, perhaps?

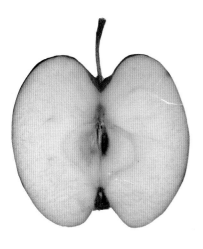

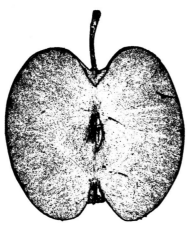

Figure 1.   Figure 2.   Figure 3.

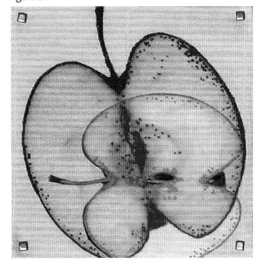

Figure 4.

The choice of fabric is perhaps the easiest part of my projects. I mostly use 100-percent woven cotton, canvas duck cloth, dupioni silk, or hemp. The choice of fabric is determined by how well it receives ink and paint for the finished look I intend. For instance, I use silk if I want to give the piece a reflective quality, and hemp for its uneven texture. Cotton duck receives ink the best, but its stiffness sometimes creates other obstacles.

Process for Imagery

I tend to begin each piece with several photographs I have taken in a variety of positions, perhaps stages of growth during the season, different times throughout the day and evening, or maybe from a distance or magnified. I photograph the central image itself along with the shadows it casts. Once I have a huge sampling of photos, I begin to experiment, drawing and illustrating from my photos see **(Figures 1 and 2)**. Sometimes I create drawings specifically meant to be individual tiles; other times, I create an overall, large drawing that I later cut up, removing or repositioning parts of it.

After completing several drawings, I scan my photos and drawings into my computer and manipulate them using Photoshop. Although I find the complexity of the program daunting, I mostly use it to create layers of my illustrations and photos. I layer an original drawing over the top of one of my hand-colored illustrations and photographs. By using different levels of opacity in each of the layers, I'm able to determine the intensity of the colors and create luminosity. Layering the illustrations and photos creates a sense of depth and filtered light **(Figure 3)**.

Whether I've created a large drawing or individual small drawings, I print them out on my fabric in sheets or tiled segments. Although printing on fabric has come a long way, I'm still not impressed with the color intensity or saturation I get. To highlight certain images or give them a reflective quality, I paint over the top of them. Sometimes I add additional details to the painted drawings as well **(Figure 4)**.

Finally, I cut my painting apart and stitch the blocks into "tiles." Each tile is tacked at the corners or along the sides to a whole-cloth quilt, giving the tiles additional dimension and a way to secure them to a sturdy background.

"Along Diamond Creek," 29¾" x 29¾" (76cm x 76cm). Detail, left.

Materials

- ◘ Wholecloth printed fabric or your own photo or drawing printed onto fabric
- ◘ Textile or acrylic paint
- ◘ Paintbrushes
- ◘ Iron and ironing board
- ◘ Backing fabric
- ◘ Point turner
- ◘ Sewing machine for straight stitching
- ◘ Thread
- ◘ Basic quilting and sewing supplies
- ◘ Batting (low-loft cotton or cotton mix)
- ◘ Embellishments (beads or buttons)

DIRECTIONS

STEP 1: Mix colors of paint to enhance or highlight parts of your photo-printed fabric. Consider adding colors that contrast with the photo or outlining specific images.

STEP 2: Paint your fabric. I like to paint all of one color first and then layer another color and another. Allow plenty of time for the paint to dry in between layers. To speed drying time, you can use a hair dryer or place the piece in the sun.

STEP 3: If necessary, press your fabric with a dry iron, on a medium setting. Make sure to lay a press cloth on your ironing surface and to press on the wrong side of the painted surface.

NOTE: Acrylic paint can transfer to another surface if overheated.

STEP 4: Cut your printed fabric or your fabric with the photo print into 5½" (14cm) squares.

STEP 5: Cut a backing fabric (for tiles) into 5½" (14cm) squares as well.

STEP 6: Align the photo-printed/painted fabric on the backing fabric, matching the right sides together.

STEP 7: Use a ¼" (.6cm) seam allowance and stitch around each side of the tile.

STEP 8: Slash the backing fabric approximately 2" (5cm) to turn the tile right-side out. Make sure not to slash through the painted (front) fabric.

STEP 9: Use a point turner in each corner to make sure the tile turns neatly.

STEP 10: Press the tiles from the back. Again, make sure to protect your pressing surface.

STEP 11: Cut the batting into 4½" (12cm) squares and stuff each tile with the batting.

STEP 12:. Embellish the tiles with buttons or beads to add additional texture.

The myriad surface design techniques covered in this chapter will provide you with endless opportunities for creating spectacular, one-of-a-kind fabrics. As mentioned at the beginning of this chapter, keeping a textile journal can be a handy reference guide for you to record all of your surface design experiments. Now that you've created some beautiful fabrics, it's time to put them to good use in an art quilt!

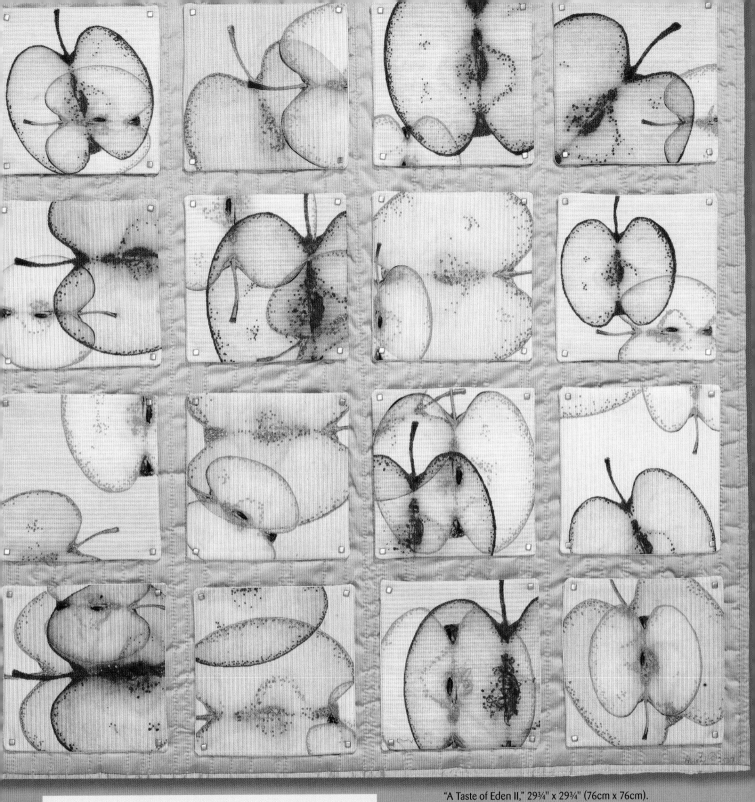

"A Taste of Eden II," 29¾" x 29¾" (76cm x 76cm).

~tip~

☞ Make sure that you try out your paint and painting tool on a test piece of your fabric to determine how much paint to load onto your tool, to see if or how much the paint bleeds, and to determine if you need to add any water or thickening agent to achieve a satisfying result.

Chapter Six
DIFFERENT TYPES OF ART QUILTS

Now that you have been exposed to art and design principles, as well as embellishment and surface-design techniques, it's time to put it all together and make some innovative quilts! Art quilts can usually be broken down into several categories: abstract quilts, pictorial or portrait quilts, and landscape quilts. If you are brand new to art quilting, it's a good idea to create small quilts so you're not overwhelmed by the size of a piece while still honing your skills. In this chapter, several master art quilters present tips and techniques for successful mastery of each type of art quilt.

"Finished Still Life," 6" W x 4" L (15cm x 10cm).

Study in a Still Life
Esterita Austin

CREATING A STILL LIFE out of fabric is a good place to start practicing your art-quilt skills. To begin this project, you'll want to first take a photograph of a still life to later interpret into fabric. There are a few basic things to think about when setting up your still-life composition for photography: strong light source, repetition, and juxtaposition.

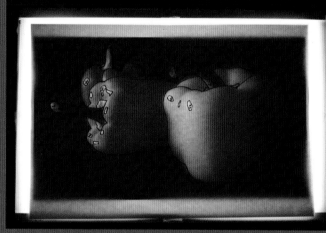
Figure 1.

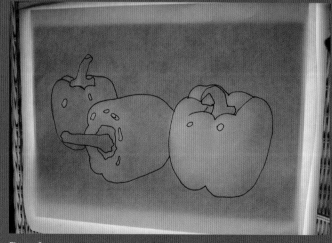
Figure 2.

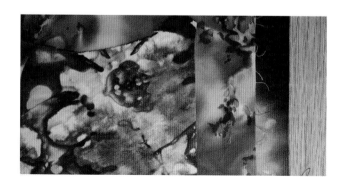
Figure 3.

Techniques to Try

Materials

- ◘ Photograph
- ◘ Rotary cutter and cutting mat
- ◘ Scissors or X-acto knife
- ◘ Sharpie marker
- ◘ Pencil
- ◘ Ballpoint pen
- ◘ Clear tape
- ◘ Assorted multi-value fabrics
- ◘ Textile paints
- ◘ White plastic plate
- ◘ Weber Museum Emerald Angle acrylic brushes in varying sizes from ¼" (.6cm) to ½" (1cm) or any suitable acrylic craft brush
- ◘ 8" x 10" (21cm x 26cm) piece of freezer paper
- ◘ 8" x 10" (21cm x 26cm) sheet of silicon-coated parchment paper or Teflon craft sheet
- ◘ 8" x 10" (21cm x 26cm) piece of black cotton fabric
- ◘ 8" x 10" (21cm x 26cm) piece of fusible webbing
- ◘ Transdoodle transfer paper or other paper for transferring

DIRECTIONS

STEP 1: Take a photograph of a still life. Vegetables provide a good study in art to practice design skills, and here I've arranged a simple still life of peppers against a backdrop of black fabric **(Figure 1)**. Set up a single light source coming from one direction. In this example, a clip-on lamp is used. This creates strong highlights on one side of the object and casts shadows on the other. Fix your camera to a tripod; if you don't have a tripod, you can brace your arms on the back of chair to steady yourself when taking the photo. Do not use a flash.

STEP 2: Print your photograph to an 8" x 10" (20cm x 25cm) size **(Figure 2)**.

STEP 3: Place an 8" x 10" (21cm x 26cm) sheet of freezer paper shiny-side down on top of your 8" x 10" (21cm x 26cm) photo. With a pencil, trace the outline of the still life onto the freezer paper **(Figure 3)**. If seeing through the freezer paper proves to be difficult, try taping your freezer-paper-covered photo to a window during daylight or use a light box for greater ease in tracing.

Transferring the Pattern to the Fabric Background

STEP 1: Tape your background fabric (in this case, black cotton) to a hard-surfaced table.

STEP 2: Centrally position and pin your freezer paper tracing on the top 2 corners, leaving the bottom corners free.

STEP 3: Lifting the unattached bottom corners of the freezer paper, slip a sheet of transfer paper such as Transdoodle between the freezer paper and the fabric.

STEP 4: On top of the freezer paper, use a ballpoint pen (pressing down with pressure) and retrace the pattern. This will transfer the design to your background fabric **(Figure 4)**. With a design as simple as this, it isn't always necessary to transfer the pattern to a background; however, if the design is more complicated, it's necessary to take this step. Transfer paper basically duplicates the drawing on fabric, upon which the cut and pre-fused fabric will be reassembled.

Choosing Fabrics

At this point the fabrics are assembled. I suggest multivalue/multicolor batiks. With more colors and a full range of values, the fabric gives more visual complexity, which enhances the image.

Layer the fabrics to be auditioned, one on top of another, on the work surface. Set aside.

Cutting the Pattern

STEP 1: Using an X-acto knife on a cutting mat, or scissors if you prefer, cut out the first template from the freezer-paper pattern **(Figure 5)**. The pattern (with the missing template) now becomes the open framework through which to view the fabric as it will appear once it's trimmed to size. It's easier to view a fabric framed within the boundaries (of an open template space) rather than try to imagine what it looks like without its boundaries.

STEP 2: With the photo for reference, move the pattern around the fabric surface, auditioning sections of the fabric to match the highlight and shadow as it appears in the photo. The color of the fabric is not a major consideration; it's all about the value. Multiple possibilities appear by moving the pattern frame around the fabric. I seldom settle on my first choice of fabric. I may pull the first layer off, revealing the layer beneath, and go searching, with the framing space, for something better.

STEP 3: Once the best fabric choice is made, place and pin the template into the empty framing space in the pattern. Place the fabric, right side up with the template pinned on top, on your cutting board. Eyeball approximately a ¼" (.6cm) of excess fabric around the template and cut with a rotary cutter or scissors **(Figure 6)**.

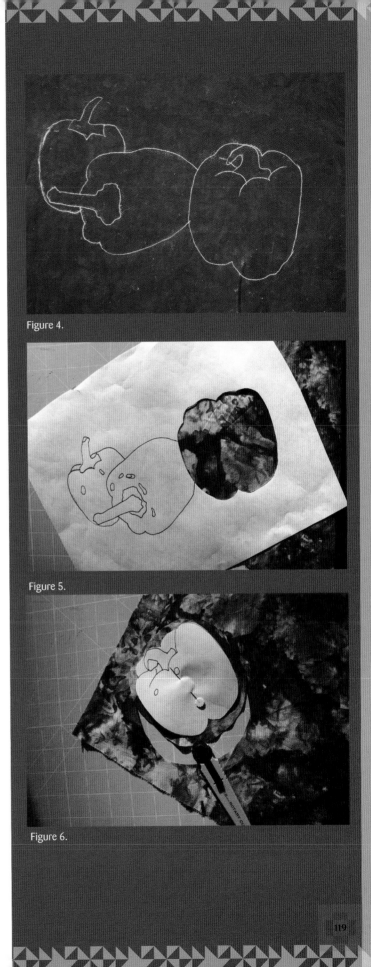

Figure 4.

Figure 5.

Figure 6.

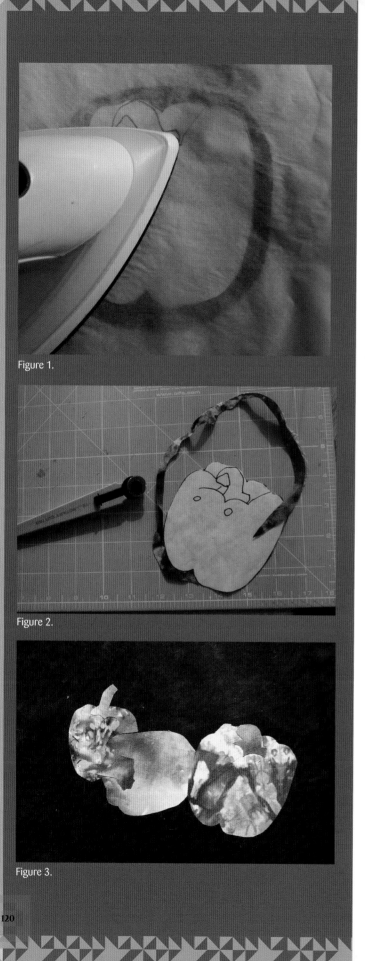

Figure 1.

Figure 2.

Figure 3.

Fusing

STEP 1: Cut the fusible approximately the same size as the background fabric.

STEP 2: Fold a piece of silicon-coated parchment paper in half (it's called baking paper or cooking paper in some parts of the world). By using parchment, your work is protected from the iron, both on top and bottom. A Teflon sheet may be used in its place.

STEP 3: Layer your pinned freezer-paper/fabric shape on a corner of the fusible webbing (release paper down). Place this "sandwich" between the folded parchment, carefully removing the pin without disturbing the arrangement.

STEP 4: Apply a hot iron (cotton setting) on the top layer of the parchment to adhere the three layers of the "sandwich" together **(Figure 1)**.

STEP 5: Once the parchment has cooled, peel the sandwich off of the parchment. Place the sandwich on your cutting mat and trim to the edge of the freezer paper **(Figure 2)**.

STEP 6: Peel the freezer paper template from the fabric and re-tape it back into the empty spot in the freezer-paper pattern. Tape the fused and trimmed fabric piece on top of the matching freezer-paper template.

STEP 7: Cut the next freezer-paper template and repeat the entire process from the beginning.

~tip~

✎ By taping first the cut and fused fabric on top of its own template, it's easy to see what the second piece—when it is being auditioned—will look like when it's viewed in direct relationship to the first. In this way, as the still life is being built, one can see exactly what one is getting.

Creating the Still Life

STEP 1: When all of the fabric pieces of the still life have been cut out and fusible webbing has been adhered to the backs, place them on the black background fabric **(Figure 3)**. If you used transfer paper such as Transdoodle to mark the placement of your pieces, make sure to brush away any visible chalk markings left from the transfer paper.

STEP 2: Once satisfied with the placement, position a new sheet of parchment on top and iron your pieces in place.

Enhancing with Paint

Paint serves as an exclamation point for the still life. It brings it to life and allows the image to visually pop off the surface.

For your paint palette, choose the same colors that appear in your fabrics. The purpose of the paint is to further enhance the value of the highlights and shadows. To create stronger highlights, tints are applied to the fabric surface. To create darker shadows, shades are applied. Both tints and shades are made in the same ratio: a dab of dark paint to the larger proportion of light paint. For instance, when making a tint of red, which would be pink, start with a larger amount of white and add a small drop of red.

When making a shade of red, again the same ratio of light to dark holds true. Start with a larger amount of the light, in this case red, and add a drop of the dark paint (either black or the complement of red, which is green) to create a deeper shade of red. A quarter- size dollop of the lighter paint is ample for a project of this size. Experiment painting on a scrap of fabric first.

Refer to the photo as reference for value placement, but allow the fabrics to dictate what happens next. Observe the patterning and textures in the fabrics. The trick is to repeat the fabric patterning in paint. Let it be the guide regarding where paint is applied. If there are small squiggly lines in the fabric, echo those lines; if there are uneven blotches, echo those. The painting should become less about making it look like the photo and more about creating an individual piece of art.

~tips~

❦ For highlighting, use tints of the colors in the fabric, as well as pure white, to lighten the side of the object.

❦ On the dark side of the object, choose the same colors but make shades darker to deepen the value.

❦ Adding paint to the medium values in the fabric is usually not necessary.

❦ The amount of paint on your brush and the pressure with which you apply it are equally important. If you load your brush with paint and put greater pressure on your brush when applying the paint, you will get full coverage on the fabric. The less paint on the brush and the less pressure of the hand, the more you can create subtle shading or fading out.

❦ If you slip and paint on your black background fabric by mistake, not to worry; that's why black Sharpie markers were invented!

❦ If your rotary blade isn't as sharp as it could be when cutting and you have a ragged edge, Sharpie marker to the rescue! Just color any frayed edges black so they blend with the background.

If you apply all of these techniques to a multipiece still-life composition, you can completely cover the surface of your background with an exciting three-dimensional image. When all is said and done, you will have an image that visually jumps off the surface.

Making Portraits
Maria Elkins

I LOVE PHOTOGRAPHS OF PEOPLE. I am always drawn to their faces, their emotions, and the repeated curves of their hair. I love to draw and paint portraits, too, but that takes time and patience, something I often have in short supply. For the last several years, I have been exploring faster, easier ways to make fabric portraits. Here is a fun and quick way to create unique postcard-size portraits of your loved ones.

Techniques to Try

Materials

- ◘ Favorite photo
- ◘ Photo-editing software program
- ◘ 2 to 3 pieces of 4" x 6" (10cm x 15cm) Steam-A-Seam2 Lite
- ◘ 3 to 4 pieces of 4½" x 6½" (12cm x 17cm) fabric, gradating from light to dark
- ◘ 1 piece of 4½" x 6½" (12cm x 17cm) solid color fabric for backing
- ◘ 1 piece of 4½" x 6½" (12cm x 17cm) stabilizer like Timtex or Peltex
- ◘ Small scissors with sharp, pointed tips
- ◘ Iron
- ◘ Sewing machine
- ◘ Invisible thread
- ◘ Coordinating decorative thread

Preparing Your Digital Picture

These directions assume you have a basic photo-editing program with the ability to crop, re-size, convert to grayscale, and posterize an image.

DIRECTIONS

STEP 1: Choose a photo of your favorite person. Ideal pictures have good contrast (strong lights and darks) and are already fairly close up (such as a head-and-shoulders shot). Candid snapshots work great **(Figure 1)**!

STEP 2: Mirror image your picture if it is important for your finished postcard to be the same orientation as your original photo.

STEP 3: Focus on one section of the face, such as just the eyes and nose, or just the mouth, and crop very closely. The cropped area should be a horizontal rectangle that is 50 percent wider than it is tall.

NOTE: Close cropping gives your finished artwork an element of surprise and a feeling of intimacy. The added bonus of close cropping is that it creates larger shapes, which makes it easier for you to cut out the pieces later.

STEP 4: Resize your cropped picture so it is 4" x 6" (10cm x 15cm). Some additional minor cropping may be necessary.

STEP 5: Convert your color photo to grayscale. If there doesn't seem to be enough contrast, make adjustments to enhance the light and dark areas.

STEP 6: Posterize your image so there are only three (or four) shades of gray in your image. Again, if the orientation matters in the end, you will want to mirror your image **(Figure 2)**.

STEP 7: Print out a test image. Measure your printout to see if it is 4" x 6" (10cm x 15cm). Examine your image for very narrow lines or very small areas—both of these will be difficult to cut out later on.

STEP 8: If your picture has 3 shades of gray, print out two images on regular paper (not photo paper). If your picture has 4 shades of gray, print out 3 images. Some software allows you to print up to three 4" x 6" (10cm x 15cm) images on a single sheet of paper. Cut images apart and trim away excess paper.

STEP 9: Outline each gray area of your picture with a red marker. Smooth out any distracting curves or jagged edges, if necessary. Number each different shade of gray, with 1 being the lightest and 3 (or 4) being the darkest **(Figure 3)**.

Figure 1.

Figure 2.

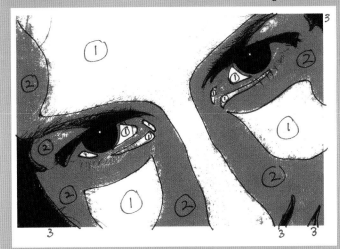

Figure 3.

Figure 4.

Figure 5.

Preparing Your Fabric Portrait

STEP 1: Choose 3 (or 4) shades of fabric. You want a definite light, medium, and dark fabric. Mentally number the fabrics, with 1 being the lightest and 3 (or 4) being the darkest. Beware of large prints. There are times when a large print adds an unexpected element that works in your favor. Other times, a large print causes you to lose important contours. It is easier to use solids, hand-dyes, or small prints.

STEP 2: Place your lightest color fabric (number 1) on top of the stabilizer and set aside.

STEP 3: Using a hot iron, press 1 rectangle of Steam-A-Seam2 Lite (SASL) to your medium color fabric (number 2). You want a good bond with the fabric, but you don't want to heat it so much that the paper backing will not come off.

STEP 4: Peel off SASL's paper backing. The SASL should be slightly tacky. Hand press your printed paper photo onto the back side of the SASL. Do not iron. You will need to remove the paper later.

STEP 5: Using the paper photo as a pattern, cut away all of the lightest areas (number 1s) of the picture from the medium fabric.

STEP 6: Remove paper photo and position your medium-color cutouts over your lightest-color fabric. If it is difficult to determine where to place the pieces, reassemble all of the medium-colored pieces like a puzzle, including the parts that will be discarded. Then carefully remove the pieces that should be discarded. Use a warm iron to press down pieces so they won't move again **(Figure 4)**.

STEP 7: Using a hot iron, lightly press 1 rectangle of SASL to your dark fabric (number 3).

STEP 8: Peel off SASL's paper backing. Hand press your printed paper photo to back side of SASL. Do not iron **(Figure 5)**.

STEP 9: Using the paper photo as a pattern, cut away the light and medium areas (numbers 1 and 2) of the picture.

STEP 10: Remove the paper photo and position over the light and medium colors.

STEP 11: Repeat if you have a fourth color.

STEP 12: Once all of the colors are aligned correctly, press with a hot iron.

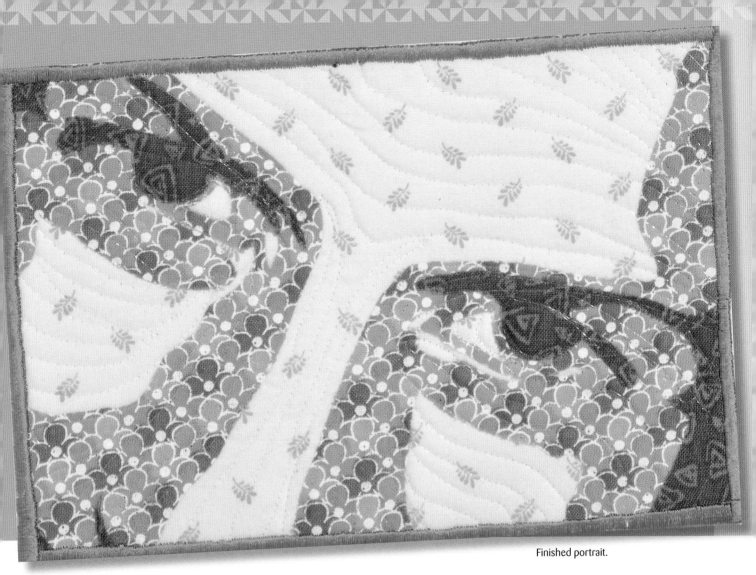

Finished portrait.

Assembly

STEP 1: Lower the feed dogs on your sewing machine and install the free-motion foot.

STEP 2: Using invisible thread, stitch through all layers of fabric and stabilizer. To enhance the three-dimensionality of the face, stitch curving parallel lines following the facial contours. Be sure to stitch close to the raw edges. If you want a different look, just stitch a pattern of straight lines or stipple over the entire face.

STEP 3: Fuse backing fabric to the back of the stabilizer.

STEP 4: Trim away the uneven edges so that the finished size is 4" x 6" (10cm x 15cm).

STEP 5: Raise the feed dogs on your sewing machine and install your standard foot (or a zigzag foot, if you have one).

STEP 6: Adjust your sewing machine to stitch a wide, very short zigzag stitch. Position your postcard so that when the needle swings to the right it will fall just past the edge of the postcard.

STEP 7: Using a decorative thread, satin stitch all 4 sides, completely covering the raw edges. With some sewing machines, it is best to zigzag a second time over the top of the first row of zigzag stitching so that the edge is completely covered.

"Pathways 1," 29" x 29" (74cm x 74cm).

The Heartfelt Landscape

Rose Hughes

HAVE YOU EVER LOOKED at a beautiful scene or imagined a fanciful design and thought to yourself, There's no way I could ever sew all those curves? Think again, and read on.

"Through the Woods," 17½" x 17½" (44cm x 44cm).

I started experimenting with curves about ten years ago, the first time I saw the sinuous lines of the hills along California's Big Sur coast. They called my name, and I soon made the move from the East Coast to the West Coast. Now the coastline's flowing curves and the color and texture of the inland hills and trees have become a treasured part of my life. I enjoy hiking and photography, so it was natural that I began to use my photographs and my memories to create my quilts, and after several years I found a way to sew those curves.

At first view, the landscapes of my heart beckon me with their vast expanses of color; then, as I look closer, the details begin to glimmer and draw me in. To capture this interplay between far and near, I began to think of the landscape in layers. The simplified shapes that make up the quilt top use fabrics in strong colors that are meant to catch your eye. Colorful yarns are then couched and combined with machine quilting to give another dimension to the design and lay the groundwork for the finer details of the hand-stitching and embellishments. Curves and circles became easy to feature in my quilts by using my Fast-Piece Appliqué method, which combines simple straight-stitch piecing methods with machine appliqué to produce shapes that would normally be very difficult to piece.

Photographs are only jumping-off points for the design process, but each quilt ends up being a combination of elements from the photographs and my feelings about the landscape. This helps my landscapes go beyond reality and convey my impressions. I believe everyone's landscapes should be expressions of her own vision.

Techniques to Try

Materials

- Photos
- Black-and-white copies of each of the photos
- Tracing paper
- Pencil, eraser, and permanent black marker
- Freezer paper
- Masking tape
- Scissors (paper, fabric, and appliqué)
- Fabric (cotton, silk with lightweight iron-on interfacing applied, or any specialty fabrics may be used; all should be able to be ironed)
- Iron and ironing board
- Sewing machine
- Thread (cotton and decorative)
- Basic quilting and sewing supplies
- Backing fabric
- Batting (lightweight, cotton, or cotton mix)
- Safety pins
- Decorative yarns (wools, cottons, or blends)

OPTIONAL MATERIALS

- Embellishments (beads, buttons, and perle cottons)
- Handsewing supplies

Creating the Pattern

I start with a general idea of a landscape that I want to create and pull out new photographs or older images from my collection to use.

Above: Original photograph.

Right: Photograph converted to black and white to enhance contrast.

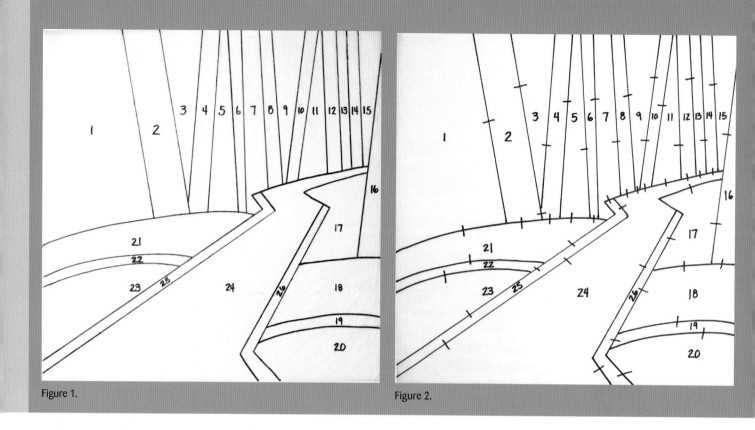

Figure 1.

Figure 2.

DIRECTIONS

STEP 1: Using the permanent marker on the copy of your photograph, select and draw around each of the basic shapes that make up the scene. Simplify complex shapes; leave details out. These make wonderful additions later on when you quilt or embellish the piece.

STEP 2: On 1 piece of tracing paper, mark an outline of the basic format of your desired quilt. Copy this onto several additional sheets of tracing paper.

STEP 3: Overlay 1 piece of tracing paper on top of the photocopy. Using a pencil, select and trace some of the various shapes you marked on the photocopy. Don't worry if this is not the perfect composition yet. This is just the starting point.

STEP 4: Overlay another sheet of tracing paper on the first. Using the first drawing as a guide, continue to create your composition. Be selective, enlarge, simplify, add, or eliminate various shapes. Continue using this drawing or add tracing paper overlays until you have the composition that you like. Remember, you may refer back to the original photo to help add details, break up larger shapes, or provide depth.

Cutting the Pattern

Once you have the design you want to use, you can move on to preparing and sewing the top.

DIRECTIONS

STEP 1: Cut a piece of tracing paper to the size of your finished quilt. Now enlarge your composition and draw it full size onto the tracing paper with pencil. Make any desired corrections or changes and then go over the pencil lines using a permanent marker. With all of the shapes copied onto the tracing paper, number each shape (1, 2, 3 . . . 26). **(Figure 1)**.

STEP 2: Cut a piece of freezer paper to the same dimensions as the tracing paper drawing. Place the freezer paper over the tracing-paper pattern. Using a permanent marker, trace the lines and numbers onto the freezer paper. Now add hash marks **(Figure 2)**. The freezer-paper drawing is now the pattern that will be used for sewing, and the tracing paper drawing is the layout guide.

STEP 3: Select the fabric you would like to use for each pattern piece. Use the tracing paper drawing as a guide to audition your fabrics. Lay them out, folded up to a reasonably accurate size, and swap them out until you're happy. It can get rather confusing to keep track of all of your fabric selections, so make squares of masking tape with numbers corresponding to the pattern pieces. Make your fabric choices and place a masking tape number on the selected fabric.

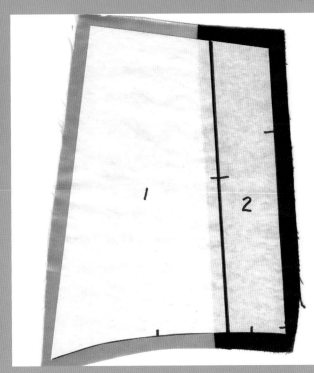

Figure 3.

"Convergence," 23" W x 47" L (59cm x 120cm).

STEP 4: With fabrics selected, it is now time to cut apart the freezer-paper pattern by cutting directly on the lines. Match up the numbered pattern piece to the chosen fabric.

STEP 5: Take the whole stack of fabrics and pattern pieces to the ironing board and iron each freezer paper pattern piece (shiny-side down) to the right side of the corresponding fabric.

NOTE: Freezer paper is first used to create the pattern and later to hold the pieces of the pattern in place to allow a high level of accuracy while you sew everything together. This also holds the fabric grain solid throughout the sewing process, eliminating the need for pins or easing a curve.

STEP 6: With the pattern piece ironed in place, cut each pattern piece from the fabric, leaving ½" (1cm) allowance all around. As you cut them, lay the pattern pieces back down onto the tracing-paper drawing.

STEP 7: Prepare for sewing by selecting 2 adjacent pattern pieces, and place them side by side on the ironing board. Butt and align the lines of the pattern pieces together using the hash marks on the pattern pieces. Once lined up, lift up the edge of 1 of the freezer-paper pattern pieces and, leaving only the width of a sewing machine needle between the edges, iron the freezer paper into place.

STEP 8: With your machine set up for straight stitching, with a neutral thread in the needle and bobbin, sew along the line left between the pattern pieces **(Figure 3)**.

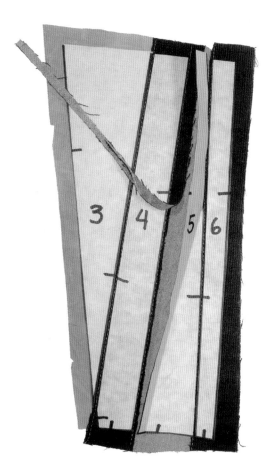

Figure 4.

Finishing

The last layer is where you make your landscape shine by adding embellishments. Embellishments can be a delightfully creative way to add dimension, texture, whimsy, and sparkle to your quilt story. Almost anything goes—beads and buttons added one at a time or on strings by hand or machine; silk ribbon, perle cottons, or decorative threads added by sewing traditional and nontraditional embroidery stitches; bangles, found objects, personal trinkets and treasures, and even paper—no matter what your choices are, you will have had fun and created your own heartfelt landscape.

Figure 5.

STEP 9: After sewing the 2 pieces together, lift up the edge of the pattern piece enough to trim back the excess fabric on the right side of the quilt. Use appliqué scissors and trim as close to the sewing line as possible. Do not trim back any of the seams on the back. Once trimmed, iron the freezer paper back into place **(Figure 4)**.

STEP 10: Continue to sew the pattern pieces together in sections, then sew the sections together until complete. Once your quilt top is sewn together, the first layer of your landscape is now done.

STEP 11: Carefully remove all the freezer paper and layer the top, batting, and backing fabric, and prepare as usual for quilting. Keep the pieces together using safety pins.

STEP 12: Couch the sewing lines of the quilt top with decorative yarns. The couching performs double duty by finishing raw edges while quilting the basic contours of the design. So as you select your yarns, choose fun colors and ones that will cover the stitching lines on the quilt top. Choose needle thread that gives extra sparkle, and remember that whatever thread is in your bobbin will appear on the back of your quilt **(Figure 5)**.

Detail of "Canyon Music March."

Designing a Landscape

Laura Cater-Woods

There are a few key things to keep in mind when designing a landscape piece:

* Where is the viewer in relationship to what is seen?
The way you divide the space will help determine this. For example, a horizontal division in thirds can indicate a horizon line and a sense of distance. Objects will be larger in the bottom of the composition and decrease in size as they recede in the distance. On the other hand, if the viewer is in the midst of things there may be no shift in size or scale to indicate distance or perspective.

* What is the mood of the time of day, season, climate, location?
Colors and values can suggest everything from dawn in a misty place to the bright clear light of midday in a dry climate. Trust your eye to choose consistently.

* Do you want to depict a realistic scene or evoke a more fanciful or abstract impression of place? If you are after a whimsical feeling, combining objects and colors without paying strict attention to size and scale relationships can work quite well. You can make choices that evoke the sense of time and place you are after, rather than worrying about realism.

If you prefer a more representational approach, it is important to choose what to keep and what to leave out. Your selections of color, texture, and detail will convey the image effectively if the details relate to each other properly. Size, scale, and value will all be important as you combine the elements to tell the viewer what is important about the scene. It is not necessary (or desirable) to try to capture all the specific details as in photo-realism.

When we work with abstraction, we have an infinite number of choices. To abstract a landscape means that key elements are suggested by use of color, composition, or perhaps a combining of materials in such a way that a sense of time and place is suggested. The artist is not bound by the details a camera might capture. The challenge is to give the viewer just enough information that her eye and imagination are engaged.

131

"Ridge 10," 27" W x 43" L (69cm x 109cm).

The Art of Abstraction

Liz Berg

PERHAPS YOU ARE EAGER TO DO AN ORIGINAL, abstract "art quilt," but you just aren't sure where to start or exactly how to do it. You probably have lots of photographs that would make a great jumping-off point for an art quilt, but to create a real piece of art, you must keep in mind the elements of design. This includes line, shape, value, color, movement, size, and pattern.

In the design process, we make all sorts of decisions about the art we are going to create. When abstracting from a photograph, we must look at the photograph and decide which elements to keep. Then, for each element, we have to choose where to put it, how to place it, what color to make it, and if we should repeat the element. This is the time to do the problem solving, using the principles of design to help you convey what you want your audience to see and feel.

Using these principles does not take away your artistic freedom. In fact, by becoming familiar with them and using them regularly, your job as the artist becomes much easier. (Of course, there are always times when you break the rules.) The principles of design are not hard-and-fast rules, but how you apply them will definitely affect the outcome of your work.

First, decide on a format. You might choose a rectangle (vertical or horizontal), a square, a circle, a narrow rectangle like a scroll, or a wide rectangle. Next, decide where to put the "horizon" point that provides focus for the other elements and for the viewer. It may be low or high, it may be made up of multiple or even vertical lines, or you may use a zigzag, spiral, or circular shape to define that horizon.

Once you have determined your format, it's time to review the elements of design.

Line

A line can be thick or thin, smooth, jagged, contoured, aggressive, calm, agitated, fast, or slow. The line brings energy to our art. Take a good look at lines in magazines, in other people's art, and in life around you, and notice how the line sends out a message to you.

Shape

Arranging shapes within a format is how we create the design of our piece. When we put an object into our piece, we have put in positive space. But the negative space—all the area around the positive space—is just as important. Adjusting the positive and negative space and the placement of multiple shapes creates not just pattern but mood, lending the piece formality, tension, looseness, and other feelings.

Value

Value is how light or dark something is. Black and white are at the opposite ends of the value scale, with black being lowest and white being highest. Pieces that have low value changes are more restful and relaxing, while those with strong value changes make a much stronger statement. Take a look at the fabric you have collected. Many of us tend to collect within a one- or two-value range and ignore the rest. For instance, do you have mostly light and medium fabrics, or do you tend toward the mediums and darks? Fabrics or art pieces with a range of value changes from light to medium to dark create a more upbeat scheme (think of a cheerful, multicolored floral). On the other hand, sticking with colors of similar values in the same piece can feel moody.

Color

Color is probably the most expressive part of the design. Study color and learn about its characteristics: hue (pure color), shade (color with black added), tint (color with white added), and tone (colors with gray added). For example, country colors are consistently made up of tones, whereas primary colors are pure hue. Also look at your colors from the point of view of warmth or coolness. Your choice of color palette is one of the most noticeable elements of your design.

Movement

Movement creates life within our work. Movement is about how the eye travels around your piece. Horizontal movement conveys a feeling of calm and restfulness, while vertical movement suggests growth (think of redwood trees) and stability.

Scale

Size matters in art; it is the scale that gives us information about the relationship of shapes within our piece. Something big feels closer, while something smaller feels farther away.

Pattern

Pattern brings everything together, using lines, shapes, values, colors, size, and textures to create a more interesting surface, which, in turn, adds to the movement in your piece.

Technique to Try

Materials

- ◘ Photograph
- ◘ Tracing paper and pencil (or photo-editing software that can turn your photo into a line drawing)
- ◘ Timtex or other strong interfacing
- ◘ Fusible webbing such as Wonder-Under or Mistyfuse
- ◘ Sewing machine and free-motion foot
- ◘ Iron and ironing board
- ◘ Hand-dyed fabrics
- ◘ Machine threads
- ◘ Dyed cheesecloth or other embellishments

OPTIONAL MATERIALS
- ◘ Joen Wolfrom's 3-in-1 Color Tool
- ◘ Black cotton duck
- ◘ Artist's stretcher bars

Practice Making an Abstraction of a Photograph

In order to change a simple picture into an interesting art piece, we will start with the element of line. In my example, notice several horizon lines, including the tops of the mailboxes and the bottom edge of the grass. Also note the vertical lines topped with various shapes.

DIRECTIONS

STEP 1: Begin by cropping the photo, turning it into a horizontal rectangle, thus moving the horizon line to the top one-third of the picture. This change puts all of the vertical elements in the lower two-thirds of the picture, making it far more interesting.

STEP 2: Lay a piece of tracing paper over the picture and trace the main elements of your design. Alternatively, you can use editing software to remove the color in your photo and reduce it to a line drawing.

STEP 3: Choose your background piece. I am starting with a dyed piece of fabric with 2 colors, neither of which is found in the original picture. This picture shows a repetitive element marching across the top half of the piece with some vertical elements along the bottom.

STEP 4: To abstract the row of mailboxes, I took the image down to the bare bones.

STEP 5: Determine the placement of the shapes. As they are placed a bit randomly to a grid, the image looks casual, rather than formal as it would if the shapes were placed at an equal distance from one another. I gave thought to which shapes would be tilted toward the center and which would tilt toward the outside. Those shapes on the left tilt just slightly outward and the right edges tilt inward, so that the eye doesn't move off of the piece. Placing the shapes of the boxes unevenly gives more movement to the piece. It also makes a strong horizontal line with strong vertical lines beneath.

STEP 6: Fuse the shapes down. I like to use Timtex as a base for my smaller pieces, as it can take a lot of stitching without causing the "quilt" to ripple. It also allows me to leave spaces unquilted if I like. I have fused my background fabric to the Timtex and have fused the shapes to the background fabric using fusible web. Because this is an art piece and not something to cuddle up with, don't worry about how stiff it becomes. In fact, the stiffness makes it easy to display on a small easel on a tabletop.

STEP 7: Do some free-motion stitching to outline shapes and some quilting for added definition and texture. I also put in something that represents grasses in several colors to add more interest to the bottom half.

STEP 8: To complete this little abstraction, finish with a satin stitch, stitching it onto black cotton duck, and stretch it over artist's stretcher bars.

✳ ✳ ✳

Hopefully these art quilt projects have inspired you to transform your ideas into one-of-a-kind art quilts. Remember that you aren't expected to make a masterpiece on your first try, nor can you expect to make the perfect art quilt every time you sit down at your sewing machine. Take it from me: it takes a lot of practice (and a fair amount of trial and error) until you get it just right. Have fun!

Fused shapes placed a bit randomly and unevenly to a grid to suggest movement and a more casual feel.

Free-motion stitching with black thread outlines the mailboxes and adds texture.

More free-motion stitching with green threads to further define the grass.

Completed abstraction finished with a satin stitch and mounted onto stretched black cotton duck.

THERE'S NOTHING WORSE than being in your creative zone, in the throes of a quilting project, when you realize you are missing the essential tools to complete it. Just as Martha Stewart recommends keeping some staple ingredients in your kitchen pantry at all times, I suggest you maintain a stash of quilting tools and supplies in your quilting studio. When you're running low, you may want to replenish your stash to a level with which you feel comfortable so you don't find yourself in a fix.

Every quilter should have and maintain a basic set of sewing and quilting tools and items on hand, including:

* **Sewing machine with free-motion stitching capabilities and sewing feet**
  Purchasing a sewing machine is such a personal and important decision. I recommend going to a national quilt show where multiple sewing machine companies are represented and trying the machines out to see which brand/model you feel most comfortable with.

* **Rotary cutters, mats, and a variety of acrylic quilting rulers**

* **Color wheel**

* **Fabric scissors, embroidery scissors, and paper scissors**

* **Sketchbook and drawing tools**

* **Variety of battings**

* **Straight pins**

* **Tweezers**

* **Hoops to keep fabric taut for hand and machine stitching**

* **Assorted machine threads in various weights and types, including monofilament, cotton, rayon, variegated, metallic**

* **Set of 80/12 universal sewing machine needles and other machine needles you use on a regular basis**
  It is recommended that you change your sewing needle frequently. (Almost every time I sit down to sew, I insert a fresh needle.) Be sure to check your sewing machine manual to use the correct needle for the fabric you're working with.

* **Spare bobbins, prefilled and empty**

* **Marking pens or pencils**

* **Tape measure**

* **Freezer paper**

* **Fabric stabilizers**
  Sulky makes a variety of tear-away, cut-away, wash-away, and heat-away stabilizers, all of which I keep on hand at all times. Each stabilizer has a different purpose. For instance, there are stabilizers designed to work with digitized machine embroidery and stabilizers designed simply to back a lightweight, flimsy fabric so the fabric doesn't get tangled in the feed dogs.

* **Spray adhesives**
  I use temporary spray adhesive (Such as 505 Spray and Fix) frequently in my work. I find it's easier to spray fabrics with a temporary adhesive than to baste with pins and also find the spray an easy way to adhere fabrics temporarily when auditioning them together on a design wall.

* **Iron and ironing board**
  I have a top-of-the-line Rowenta I use for piecing, but for daily activities such as fusing fabrics and Angelina fibers, heat setting paints and the like, I use an inexpensive iron. That way if I accidentally get fusible or paint on the iron, I'm not going to beat myself up over it.

* **Teflon pressing sheet or a roll of parchment paper to protect your ironing board when fusing Angelina fibers and fabrics**

* **Tracing paper**

* **Fabrics**
  HAND-DYED FABRICS
  I recommend purchasing hand-dyed fabrics or dyeing fabrics in all colors and hues of the color wheel. At a minimum, I try to maintain a fat quarter of each hue. I keep a list of what I am low on so the next time I am at a quilt show, I can replenish my stash.

  COMMERCIAL FABRICS
  Similarly, I try to maintain a stash of fabrics with various prints in each hue. Katie Pasquini Masopust once noted that quilters tend to buy medium-hued fabrics rather than lights and darks. It's those light and dark fabrics that make bold fabrics pop, so it's important to maintain your stash. And remember, quilters, there is no such thing as having too much fabric!

The following is a list of additional items and tools that are great to have on hand but not always necessary.

* **9" x 12" (23cm x 31cm) sheets of Kunin felt**
I keep a stash of these inexpensive felt sheets next to my sewing machine and use them to warm myself up for free-motion stitching. Kunin felt is also synthetic, and hence melts and burns when extreme, concentrated heat such as that from a heat gun is applied—ideal for creating burned effects. (Natural wool felt does not burn.) Usually when I go to a craft store, I'll buy the entire stash they have on the shelf because these felt sheets are so inexpensive and versatile.

* **Digital camera, printer, printable fabric sheets**

* **Fusibles**
WONDER-UNDER BY PELLON
Wonder-Under is a fusible webbing of glue backed on nonstick "release" paper used traditionally to fuse fabrics. The fusible webbing glue melts and adheres to the fabric when heat is applied by an iron. When it has cooled, the release paper is pulled away, leaving the fusible glue on the fabric. Wonder-Under comes on a bolt and is available at fabric, quilting, and many major craft stores.

MISTYFUSE
I also use Mistyfuse fusible webbing quite a bit. It has a lighter hand than Wonder-Under and is ideal for more delicate fabrics as well as for quilts where you want to maintain a more supple feel. (Wonder-Under has a tendency to make quilts stiffer. Sometimes this is the desired effect wanted for art quilts.)

BO-NASH 007 BONDING AGENT
Bo-Nash consists of little salt-like crystals of fusible webbing you can sprinkle sparsely or liberally to fuse fabrics and fibers to your artwork.

* **A set of fine-tipped Pigma pens in different colors**
These fine felt-tipped markers are perfect for writing on fabric. I often use them for writing my labels on the backs of quilts. Yvonne Porcella also taught me a trick years ago: If you want to camouflage a machine stitching mistake (for instance, if you went outside the line), you can try coloring your stitched thread with a Pigma pen the color of the background fabric.

* **Craft heat gun**
Many art quilters are experimenting with burning and melting synthetic fabrics, and a craft heat gun (available at craft and stamping stores) is a good tool to have on hand. Be sure that when you use the heat gun, you are working outside or in a well-ventilated area.

* **Decorative trims, yarns, and ribbons**

* **Embellishments**
You probably have more of an embellishment stash on hand than you realize: buttons, seed beads and charms, found objects, etc. You'll never look at anything at a garage sale, flea market, or on eBay the same way again!

* **Fabric paints, including metallic paints**

* **Set of Shiva Paintstiks**
These are highly pigmented oil sticks loaded with vibrant color that can be used on fabric. They are wonderful for stenciling and adding dense color and metallic shimmer.

* **Stencils and stamps**

* **Angelina fusible fibers**
These shiny, plastic fibers are light-refractive. They create a gossamer, shimmering piece of fabric when fused together with an iron on the silk setting.

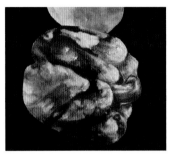

Natalya Aikens's art is an exploration of her heritage. Although Natalya has been fully integrated into the American way of life for more than twenty-five years, she feels her Russian heritage pulling at her heart strings, and she must express it through her art. You can see Natalya's work at artbynatalya.com.

Esterita Austin is an internationally award-winning quilt maker, designer, and teacher. Her work has been widely shown in international museums and galleries, as well as published in magazines and books. The use of textural and dimensional imagery has given Esterita's work a unique style. See more of her work at esteritaaustin.com.

Dina Buckey is an art quilter and wearable artist who recently relocated to Brandenburg, Kentucky. Dina is a member of SAQA, Carnegie Art Quilt Alliance, and the Louisville Area Fiber and Textile Artists. She can be reached at dina@catlover.com.

Jane Dunnewold produces more than 100 unique lengths of fabric every year and is an advocate of art cloth. She maintains Art Cloth Studios in San Antonio, Texas. Visit her at complexcloth.com.

Pamela Allen is a full-time artist in Kingston, Ontario, Canada. She travels, shows, and teaches workshops in Canada and the United States. When not making art quilts, Pamela is haunting dollar stores and thrift shops for fabrics and unique objects for embellishments. See her work at pamelart2.homestead.com/quiltythings.html.

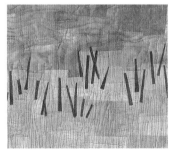

Liz Berg is a full-time professional studio artist working in fiber. Her work has been in many juried art, fiber, and quilt shows and is represented by several galleries. Liz speaks at guilds and retreats and teaches classes on color, design, surface design, and beginner art quilting. You may view her work at lizbergartquilts.com.

Laura Cater-Woods is a compulsive mark-maker, currently working in mixed media and fiber. Her abstract imagery explores textures, rhythms, and details from the landscape, often interwoven with eccentric grids. Visit Laura's website at cater-woods.com or email her at lcaterw@msn.com.

Robbi Joy Eklow enjoys working with fiber and using it as a way to introduce herself to people. She makes art quilts from cotton fabrics that she dyes herself, using bonded appliqué and free-motion quilting. Robbi enjoys lecturing and teaching and sharing her techniques to encourage others to find their voice through fiber. Visit robbieklow.com.

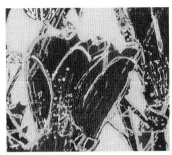

Maria Elkins is passionate about fabric. She is fascinated with ethnic and historical clothing, weaving, feltmaking, and papermaking. Throughout all her investigations, quiltmaking is the one medium that has captivated and consumed her. Visit her at mariaelkins.com.

Julie Hirota is an award-winning artist who also lectures, teaches, and creates commissions for residential and corporate clients throughout the United States. She resides in Roseville, California, with her husband and her two young children. See more of her work at jhiro.com or contact her at julie@jhiro.com.

Rose Hughes is a fabric artist from Southern California who creates one-of-a kind quilt art pieces, where color and shape play with the senses. Rose lectures and teaches many of the techniques she has written about. Visit Rose's website at rosehughes.com.

Lyric Kinard's award-winning wall quilts and wearable works of art are a product of her need and passion to create order and beauty while living a chaotic life as the mother of five young children. Her second love is teaching, which she has been doing in various capacities for the past 12 years. Visit her website at lyrickinard.com.

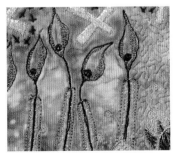

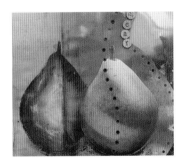

Deana Hartman is an artist who creates original designs sculpted by fabric, extensive free-motion quilting, and beaded embellishment. Her works reflect diverse topics from the spiritual realm to nature to technology. Her art quilts can be found in corporate as well as private collections across the United States and Canada. Visit her website at chameleonquilts.com.

Angie Hughes is a textile artist and tutor who lives and works in Ledbury, Herefordshire, United Kingdom. She currently teaches in her studio, Ledbury Artplace, and for guilds and groups all over the country. Visit her website at angiehughes.com.

Linda and Laura Kemshall, as Design Matters, work together full-time making quilts for exhibition and teaching City & Guilds design-based creative programs through their website sixart.co.uk. The artists can be reached through lindakemshall.com.

Holly Knott is an artist who spends her free time working in a wide variety of media. Her photographs and art quilts have won awards and are exhibited in juried art exhibits and quilt shows nationally. You can view Holly's work at hollyknott.com.

Katy Korkos made the transition to fiber artist after many art classes and after moving to New Mexico, where it is hard not to be an artist. She lives with her husband, David, in Los Alamos, New Mexico, where she works as a journalist. More of her work can be seen at web.mac.com/katykorkos.

Heidi Lund is an artist with a passion for fabric, fiber, and surface embellishments. She makes wearable art, art quilts, and beaded jewelry and has been exhibited nationally and internationally. Heidi teaches quilting, surface design, collage, dyeing, embellishment, and beading. Visit heidilund.com.

Linda S. Schmidt is a quilter, teacher, mother, secretary, writer, and musician. Linda's business is called Short Attention Span Quilting. She has been teaching and exhibiting for the last thirteen years, nationally and internationally, and is a member of the faculty of the online quilting academy, quiltuniversity.com. To see more of her artwork, visit shortattn.com.

Beryl Taylor is the author of *Mixed-Media Explorations* and imaginatively manipulates, dyes, paints, stamps, embroiders, and decorates her papers and fabrics to produce enriching textured effects with vibrant colors. An enduring theme in Beryl's work is the incorporation of the heart motif, which is, in her own words, a reflection of her love for her art. More of her work can be viewed at beryltaylor.com.

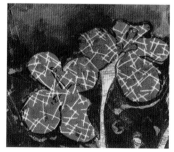

Charlotte Liddle is a textile designer who specializes in embroidery with interesting combinations of color, pattern, and texture. A graduate of The University of Huddersfield in the United Kingdom, Charlotte has her own design business and also teaches a variety of textile workshops. To learn more about Charlotte, visit her website at charlotteliddle.com.

Judy Coates Perez is well-known for her highly detailed, colorfully painted, wholecloth quilts. Her extensive travels have influenced the diversity of her work, which explores themes drawn from folklore, history, and nature. You can see more of her work and read about her creative process at judyperez.blogspot.com.

Lucie Summers finds the inspiration for her work from a diverse mixture of sources. She loves living in the country and tends to use a lot of leaf and floral motifs in her work. She favors frayed and rough edges and likes the idea of things changing, fading over time. Lucie can be reached at lucie-summers@yahoo.co.uk.

Melanie Testa graduated from the Fashion Institute of Technology in New York City with a degree in textile/surface design. Soon after graduation she began to pursue her love of fabric: painted, sewn, beaded, embellished, and surface-designed. Her work can be seen at melanietesta.com.

Laura Wasilowski is both a contemporary quiltmaker and a creator of hand-dyed fabrics and threads. Laura's narrative quilts begin with unique fabrics and are inspired by stories of family, friends, and home. Owner of the dye shop Artfabrik, Laura is also a lecturer, surface designer, quilt instructor, and author. Visit artfabrik.com.

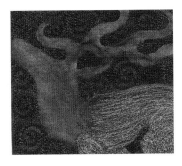

Karen Williams's mixed-media art is an exploration in color and texture, celebrating the natural world. Her work incorporates dye, paint, oil sticks, stitch, bead embellishment, and found objects. She often experiments with unexpected uses of these materials. Visit skunkhillstudio.com.

Brackman, Holly. **The Surface Designer's Handbook: Dyeing, Printing, Painting, and Creating Resists on Fabric.** Loveland, CO: Interweave Press, 2006.

Bresenhan, Karey Patterson. **Creative Quilting: The Journal Quilt Project.** Loveland, CO: Interweave Press, 2006.

Davila, Jane, and Elin Waterston. **Art Quilt Workbook: Exercises & Techniques to Ignite Your Creativity.** Lafayette, CA: C & T Publishing, 2007.

Dunnewold, Jane. **Complex Cloth: A Comprehensive Guide to Surface Design.** Woodinville, WA: Martingale & Company, 1996.

Eklow, Robbi Joy. **Free Expression: The Art and Confessions of a Contemporary Quilter.** Loveland, CO: Interweave Press, 2005.

Kemshall, Linda, and Laura Kemshall. **The Painted Quilt: Paint and Print Techniques for Color on Quilts.** Cincinnati, OH: F & W, 2007.

Lawler, Mickey. **Skydyes: A Visual Guide to Fabric Painting.** Lafayette, CA: C & T Publishing, 1999.

Michler, J. Marsha. **The Magic of Crazy Quilting: A Complete Resource for Embellished Quilting.** Iola, WI: Krause, 1998.

Shrader, Valerie Van Arsdale. **Simple Contemporary Quilts: Bold New Designs for the First-Time Quilter.** Asheville, NC: Lark Books, 2007.

Van Horn, Larkin Jean. **Beading on Fabric: Encyclopedia of Bead Stitch Techniques.** Loveland, CO: Interweave Press, 2006.

Williamson, Jeanne. **The Uncommon Quilter: Small Art Quilts Created with Paper, Plastic, Fiber, and Surface Design.** New York: Potter Craft, 2007.

Suppliers

Please contact Quilting Arts Magazine for all of your book, surface design, mixed-media, thread, fiber, stamp, stencil, gel, and rubbing plate needs.
PO Box 685
23 Gleasondale Rd.
Stow, MA 01775
quiltingarts.com

Art Van Go (U.K.)
1 Stevenage Rd.
Knebworth, Hertfordshire, UK
SG3 6AN
artvango.co.uk
Books, surface design and mixed-media supplies

Bernina of America, Inc.
3702 Prairie Lake Ct.
Aurora, IL 60504
(630) 978-2500
berninausa.com
Sewing machines and embroidery software

Dharma Trading Co.
PO Box 150916
San Rafael, CA 94915
(800) 542-5227
dharmatrading.com
Dye and paint supplies; Pébéo Setacolor, including Pébéo Setacolor Pâte Relief à Expanser Expandable Paint; PFD fabric

Dick Blick Art Materials
PO Box 1267
Galesburg, IL 61402-1267
(800) 828-4548
dickblick.com
Caran d'Ache Neocolor II Artists' Crayons, texture gels, paints, sketchbooks, and general art supplies

eQuilter.com
5455 Spine Road, Ste. E
Boulder, CO 80301
equilter.com
Wide variety of commercial fabrics, patterns, magazines, books

Fire Mountain Gems
1 Fire Mountain Way
Grants Pass, OR 97526-2373
(800) 355-2137
firemountaingems.com
A variety of beads, Swarovski crystals, pressed glass, charms, books

PRO Chemical & Dye
PO Box 14
Somerset MA 02726
(800) 228-9393
prochemical.com
Fabric paints, dyes, PFD fabric, and supplies

Jones Tones
33865 United Ave.
Pueblo, CO 81001
jonestones.com
(719) 948-0048
Puff Paint by Jones Tones

Puffy 3D Paint by Tulip
Available from most craft stores

Screen-Trans Development Company
screentrans.com
(201) 933-7800
Foil-On fabric applications

Skydyes Fabric
PO Box 370116
West Hartford, CT 06137-0116
skydyes.com
Handpainted cottons by Mickey Lawler

Testfabrics
415 Delaware Ave.
PO Box 26
West Pittiston, PA 18643
(570) 603-0432
testfabrics.com
PFD fabrics

The Thread Studio (Australia)
08 9227 1561
thethreadstudio.com
Surface design and mixed-media supplies, fibers, kits, books, stamps, magazines

USArtQuest
usartquest.com
Adhesives, embellishments, mica products, paints, pigments, paper products, books, videos

Meinke Toy
(Internet orders only)
(248) 813-9806
Meinketoy.com
Xpandaprint

Index

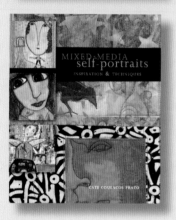
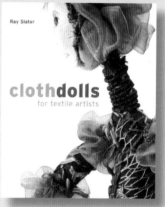